WANNA BET?

ALSO BY **ARTIE LANGE**

TOO FAT TO FISH

CRASH AND BURN

ARTIE LANGE

WITH ANTHONY BOZZA

WANNA BET?

A DEGENERATE GAMBLER'S GUIDE TO LIVING ON THE EDGE

ST. MARTIN'S PRESS ⚞ NEW YORK

The Library of Congress Cataloging-in-Publication Data is available upon request.

ISBN 978-1-250-12117-2 (hardcover)
ISBN 978-1-250-19965-2 (signed edition)
ISBN 978-1-250-18177-0 (ebook)

Our books may be purchased in bulk for promotional, educational, or
business use. Please contact your local bookseller or the Macmillan Corporate and
Premium Sales Department at 1-800-221-7945, extension 5442, or by email at
MacmillanSpecialMarkets@macmillan.com.

First Edition: July 2018

10 9 8 7 6 5 4 3 2 1

For Valdastri, Falato, Meneve, Attell, Pete and Judd, Rich Super, Jen, Norm and Frank S., of course, Mom and Stace. I love you all. And Anthony Bozza. Special thanks to Anthony C and Keith. And to Sherrod Small, I'm so sorry I haven't called you back. When my counselor in rehab told me to stay away from triggers, I misunderstood him.

CONTENTS

WANNA BET?

INTRODUCTION:

PLACE YOUR BETS

When you think about it, and lately I have, everything we do comes down to risk. Where you end up in life is all about what you are willing to do to get there. And no one gets anywhere without gambling a bit. You can go on all you want about making your own destiny by visualizing your goals, you can read *The Secret*, you can listen to self-help tapes. I encourage those of you who believe in that bullshit to keep it up, because it leaves a lot of room at the front of the line for the people with brains who believe in logic. Those people know that what you do when your life comes to a crossroad is what determines who you are. Those moments are no time to be timid, because how much you bet can make all the difference in the path your life takes.

This might sound very simplistic or black and white to some of you, but if you see it that way, you're missing the point. Risk is important, but it isn't the only factor here.

Let me put it another way. If your time on earth were to be broken down into a series of stats as if you were a baseball player, then the risks you take would be counted as one of the most important numbers you could ever post up. It wouldn't be the main number that defines your career, but it would say a lot about you. Risk wouldn't be your batting average if you were a great hitter, or your ERA if you were a great pitcher. The amount of risk you leveraged in your life would be your stolen bases or how many runners you picked off. It would be the mystery figure that slid under the radar but upon further review told the story of exactly how you played the game.

That number explains what you will do when faced with two outs in the bottom of the ninth. Whether you swing for the fences or bunt, no great success comes without great risk. If it were any other way, it wouldn't even be a game; it would be batting practice.

If you know nothing about me, then start here: I love risk, and I chase it because that rush is what keeps me going. I have taken completely comfortable situations and turned them upside down for the risk of it. That's a selfish thing to do, but it has to happen, because instability is what drives my creativity. This might seem like an excuse, but it's not; it's self-knowledge. I know that chaos is what fuels me. I am an engine that runs on it, and I keep that tank topped-up better than I do the tank in my car. I've also found that life has a funny way of keeping things unstable for me. Every time I've felt like I've had things figured out, life has thrown me a curveball, because that's what life does.

I've missed a lot of sinking curveballs, by the way, but

those whiffs aside, when I talk about risk, I'm talking about the greatest rush I've ever known—and I've known a lot of them. It's a very powerful and specific high. It's not the rush you experience when you go all-in and hit 21 at the blackjack table. Sure, that's great, but that's not it. It's not like the high you get if you win your first bet either. That's the intoxication of beginner's luck, which is actually a curse, because that will get you hooked for good if you're so inclined. I should know; I won my first bet and I've never looked back. What I'm talking about runs even deeper than that, though. It comes from a place where losing might be just as fun as winning, so in a way, you don't care about what happens as much as you care about the bet itself. Depending on how boring your life is, in some cases, losing can be even better than winning.

I placed my first bet with a bookie when I was fifteen years old. This might sound a bit early to some of you, but where I grew up in Newark, New Jersey, betting with bookies was a regular thing. My friend who was my age had an older brother who bet on sports every week, like all the older kids did. It was cool and exciting, and who didn't want to be as cool as the older kids growing up? Anyway, he got us in on the action, and once he did, I was done.

The first bet I ever placed was in January 1985, on Super Bowl XIX, the 49ers versus the Dolphins. All my buddies liked Miami and Dan Marino. Following their lead seemed boring to me, so I did the illogical thing and bet on Joe Montana and the Niners. My friends thought I was crazy. They also thought I was an asshole because I was a Giants fan, and Giants fans never, ever rooted for the Niners in the '80s. It was rivalry so deep that we didn't want them to even win a fucking coin toss. In the end, the Niners blew Miami out 38–16, and just like that, I won my first bet and I was hooked on gambling.

Winning your first bet is literally the worst thing that can happen to anyone. It's a brief victory that gives the winner a false sense of invincibility. I put fifty dollars on that game, which means that I'd get a hundred dollars if I won. To bet fifty dollars, you had to pay fifty-five dollars to cover the five-dollar vig, which is a service fee to the bookie. I won the bet and was handed a hundred bucks, which made me feel like I'd won a hundred dollars. That's the mirage: winning completely erased the memory that my initial fifty dollars was included in the prize money. It wasn't even fifty dollars! Whether I won or lost, the bookie kept the five-dollar vig, so all I could ever win was forty-five dollars. I didn't see that at all; I just thought, *This is great; I just won a hundred bucks!*

That was the start of it all for me, and it won't ever end, but I've come to terms with that. Because, you see, gambling on sports is fun, and I've done plenty of it, but I've moved on. When I was making real money, in the 1990s, I really did some damage to my income, which is why I've made about ten million over the years but am worth around two if I'm being generous. How did I do it? Well, more than once I bet twenty-five thousand on the coin toss at the Super Bowl. The odds are literally fifty-fifty, it's pure chance, which is what I love about that bet. Anyway, that kind of betting stopped doing it for me, so I moved on to a much more serious type of wager: gambling with intangible assets, like my life.

This type of risk and the thrill that comes with it is

dangerous and something most people can't fathom when I try to explain it to them. If you don't get it, don't feel bad. You should feel happy, because if what I'm saying sounds strange, there's a good chance that you're normal, adjusted, sane, and functional. Don't change who you are, because if you're curious about this state of mind, worry no more— you can live vicariously through me! I'll do my best to explain it to you in this book, but if you still don't get it, just watch the headlines, because I'm living it every day. All you need to do is follow me on Twitter @artiequitter to see examples of my risk condition in real time.

When I look back on my life, which is something you do when you're my age and realistically shouldn't be alive, it's miraculous that my philosophy has worked for me. There are many reasons for that, the first of which is that show business loves second chances (and thirds and fourths), which is how I'm still able to buy into this craps game at all. The best way to explain what drives me is that, in simplest terms, I'm into a different type of rush. I don't feel like I've done anything worthwhile until I've achieved something after risking everything, which comes from a place of not caring whether I win or lose, succeed or fail. I mean, sure I like to succeed, but success without a risk or struggle doesn't seem honest to me.

What I do when it comes to life is take risks but also make risks when there aren't any. I know it sounds careless, but if it's done right, gambling like that isn't a dive into the abyss; it's sitting on the edge, telling the abyss to kiss your ass. Doesn't that sound exciting? If it does, I'd like to tell you about some beachfront property in Appalachia that I have for sale. If chaos is your best friend, or you feel most comfortable amid instability, you probably understand my frame of mind. That still doesn't mean you're the type to go the extremes that I do. To me, risking and breaking even, or plodding along consistently, winning small, are fates worse than death. I would rather risk everything I have and lose than be bored. Luckily, I've managed to do that without making my mother or me homeless, though I have come close a few times.

I've pinpointed the moment I first caught this high. When I was nineteen, I was working construction, making about $12,000 a year. That's also when I developed a taste for booze and cocaine, which pair well with gambling if you want to cure a case of the boredoms. Anyway, one snowy Monday night I was at a bar drinking and shooting the shit with a buddy of mine. We'd spent the weekend betting on every college and NFL game, and I don't remember if we were ahead or behind, but at that point the only thing left to talk about was a Cleveland Browns game. Cleveland is a town with some degree of charm, but they've never had a strong football team. In fact, the Browns are probably the least winning, least cared-about team in the history of the NFL or professional sports for that matter. Back then I knew nothing about their players, and I still don't. The Browns are not on anyone's radar unless they are from Cleveland.

My buddy was getting ready to go home that night, but I didn't want him to, because I wasn't done with excitement. We were in a Jersey sports bar, it was cold, it was November, and it was Monday, so thrills were at a minimum. But I wouldn't accept that.

"Hey, man," I said, "how much do you have in your bank account?"

"I don't know, Art, maybe a thousand bucks?" he said.

"Great. You're not going anywhere, and here's what you're gonna do," I said. "Bet fifteen hundred on Cleveland. Kickoff is in half an hour; we still have time to call the bookie."

"Are you kidding me?" he asked.

"No."

"Art, why would I do that? I don't know anything about this game. I don't even know who coaches Cleveland."

"Exactly!"

"What are you talking about? Why the hell should I bet on them, then?"

"Listen to me," I said. "You're bored, right?"

"I mean, yeah, but come on, dude."

"Listen to me," I said. "You know nothing about this game, and neither do I. But no matter who wins, if you put fifteen hundred on the Browns to win, I can promise you one thing."

"What's that?"

"Without a doubt, the next three hours will be fucking exciting!"

My friend looked at me like he was seeing me for the first time, which in many ways he was.

"Art, you're not kidding, are you?"

"Not at all."

"Man, you're fucking crazy."

My buddy went home. I didn't. After he left, I called the bookie with five minutes to spare before kickoff.

Remember this story as you read this book if you feel like you and I might be kindred spirits. We might have a few things in common, but at our core, I'd put good money on us being very different. And that's okay. That's actually good! You don't want to be like me. I'm sure some of you are reading this and shaking your heads. Okay, fine, we're alike; you're crazy too. I get it: you gamble, you risk it all, you live on the edge. That's cool, man. But let me ask you something: Have you ever been strung out on coke, in Vegas, at 5:00 a.m., asking your fellow degenerate gamblers if they knew the score of the East Coast divisional finals in girls' high school lacrosse? Hey, man, did Connecticut win? *Did* they? *Did they?*

God, I hope you've never been there. In my nightmares I still see the awkward stares. Because they'd lost.

If you've read my other two books, you know how lucky I've been. I've also been foolish and destructive and have needed all the help and second chances I've gotten. At this point I spend my free time just trying to make sense of it all, and trying, believe it or not, to come to some sort of happy middle ground. Maybe not happy. I'll be happy enough with just middle.

I recognize that risk and thrill are the driving forces in my life, so in order to better understand myself, I've tried to pinpoint a handful of the biggest risks that have defined my life, and I plan to tell you about them in the following pages. I also plan to tell you about some of the people I grew up with and the friends I've made so you'll see other examples of risky people like me and how things turned out for them. Some risks, like skipping college to chase my dream—I'd never tell anyone not to do that. Others, like trying heroin, a drug I'd romanticized for years, I'd do anything to keep someone from following in my footsteps. Out of all my life's risks, that is the only one I wish I could take back. And if you'd like an in-depth understanding of why, read my second book, *Crash and Burn*.

So here's to a life lived in gambling, and here's to gambling with your life. I don't recommend it, but it's all I know how to do. There is no status quo for me, just a lot of highs, a lot of lows, a lot of going all-in and getting by on sleight of hand and the luck of the draw.

I

THE POT-SMOKING LAUGH

My father was a pivotal figure in my life. He was an opinionated wiseass, he was hilarious, he was hard-working, and he possessed the kind of balls and inner-city know-how that cannot be taught. As much as he could, he turned life upside down and shook the spare change from its pockets. He was active and had a lot of energy, which made his last years on earth very hard for him. After suffering a terrible accident on the job as an antenna repairman, he spent his last four years as a quadriplegic. My dad always took risks and lived according to nobody's rules, which is a trait I inherited for better and for worse. I regret nothing, and I hope I've done him proud or at least given him a lot to laugh about up in heaven. At the end of his life, when my father was in his bed, desperate to escape the pain and the fate that life had dealt him, laughs were valuable. The story I'm about to tell you was one that would make him smile when nothing else could, no matter how many times he'd heard it.

Birds of a feather flock together, so it shouldn't come as a surprise that a lot of my childhood friends were thick-headed risk takers like me. Say what you will about us, but I am still in touch with all my closest friends from high school, except the ones who died. When we were kids, all of them believed they'd go for broke and take life by the balls like I did, only they didn't actually do it. They all had big plans. A lot of them wanted to be in bands, because when I was in junior high and high school, every guy I knew wanted to be in a band. I don't think that's changed, because being in a band is still the coolest thing you can do if you're not funny enough to be a comedian.

Anyway, a few thousand kids went to my high school, and it's safe for me to admit now that out of the white kids, I wasn't even close to being the funniest. If we are counting the black kids in my high school, I wouldn't even rank in the top one hundred. Remember this, because there is a reason why I'm here and they're not. All those guys helped me develop as a comedian, and I'm thankful. My high school was probably 33 percent Italian, 33 percent Irish, 33 percent black. There were some Hispanics and exactly one Jewish kid, which I'm sure of because that kid was doomed. He was the odd man out, and to make matters worse, he wasn't Jewish enough. He lacked that instinctual, natural Jewish sense of humor that he desperately needed to fit in. He had none of it. He was, as Howard Stern would say, a *goyishe kop*, which is a Yiddish term used to refer to someone who is Jewish but isn't like a Jew. If you're a Jew, you would use this term to describe a Jewish colleague who isn't good with money, for example. Penguins and chickens, being birds who don't fly, are *goyishe kops*.

I've always loved that term, and Howard and I had this quid pro quo thing when it came to old-world Jewish and Italian terms. Howard loved a few Italian slang phrases that he picked up from me, and they weren't even insults; they were just bad Italian American bastardizations. One of his favorites was *shviadell*, which is a mutilated version of *sfogliatelle*, the word for an Italian pastry that non-Italians call a "lobster tail." I said it during a drunken toast I gave in Las Vegas the first time we did *The Howard Stern Show* out there, and he locked on to it. I got up and said something stupid like, "Salud, chindon, broccoli rabe, shviadell." None of those words aside from *salud* really have any business being in a toast, but he didn't care. I don't think he even knew; he just liked the sound of *shviadell*. That one stayed with him, and *goyishe kop* stayed with me.

The entire idea of a person who is bad at being what they were born to be is hilarious to me. It's inspiration, because that's what I am. That's what gambling is, that's what taking a risk means to me: being bad at what you are. If I were a Jew, I'd be a *goyishe kop*, because any Jew who behaves the way I do with money is a very bad Jew. It's funny when Jewish and Italian American cultures come together in unexpected ways, because at their roots, they're similar: both groups' mothers use guilt to control their children, and both groups' dominant religious institutions are controlling and hypocritical. They deal with misbehavior differently, but if you ask me, they're coming from the same place. And when they've mixed things up, some results have been innovative. The pizza-bagel isn't a bad thing when you can't get a real slice, and if it weren't for Jewish and Italian American culture coming together, we wouldn't have the Ramones, who were one of the greatest rock-and-roll groups of all time. They were a bunch of Jewish guys posing as Italian greasers who went so far as to choose a ridiculous Italian-sounding name for themselves. Joey Ramone's real last name was Hyman, for Christ's sake! The Ramones acted Italian but were very Jewish. Except for Dee Dee. He was the Ramone who always got into trouble. I'm not sure he was Jewish, because he certainly did not act Jewish. I guess he was the Ramones' *goyishe kop*. He was immortalized with a statue right at the entrance to the Hollywood Forever Cemetery for all his misbehavior, God bless him.

I was driving through my old neighborhood of Elizabeth, New Jersey, with my cousin the other day and I got to thinking about all the *goyishe kops* I grew up with, none of whom will have a statue erected in their honor. I have to say, my family's old house and everything around it looked smaller. The whole place seemed different: the neighbors used to be lighter, and I'm not talking about their weight. There used to be strike zones painted on every bare brick wall you'd pass by, and it's just not like that anymore.

We used to stay outside all night playing stickball against any number of walls until my friend Billy Hazelton's dad whistled. That was the signal and how we knew we had to go home. Everybody from Newark can do that whistle, by the way, either with their two pinkies or just their thumb and forefinger. It would be nine at night, just starting to get dark, but we'd keep playing until we heard the whistle. That meant it was time for supper.

Summer nights like that are my greatest memories of childhood, and I feel bad for these millennials that will never know what it was like being a real kid. In the summer, with no homework to do, we wouldn't see our parents for, like, fifteen hours. We'd stay outside and make up games or other things to do. We socialized by talking to each other, which, believe it or not, is what spoken language was developed for. There was no texting, no cell phones, no one sending you a fucking emoji on your birthday. There isn't an emoji that can capture how we felt and what we experienced during those summer nights. How would I have said "The Luciano brothers stole my wallet" in an emoji?

The Unlucky Luciano Brothers, as we are going to call them here, taught me more about risk and not giving a fuck than anyone else I've ever known. They gave me my first taste of it, and they were my heroes. I've changed their names, by the way, even though they're both dead; that's how much I respect them. The older brother we will call Louie (he was two years older than I was), and the one who was my age we will call Tony.

There was a place in North Newark called Two Guys Department Store (a name I will not change), which is where we used to steal things, because that's what street kids do. At that place it was easy, because the security guard was older than dirt. He was at the end of his career, capable of either that job or watching people steal burgers from White Castle. I got the feeling that he probably hadn't done anything too complicated earlier in life, which was great, because nobody who steals wants to get caught. That type of old-school department store is a thing of the past, by the way, so I'm not sure younger readers understand what those places were like. It was divided into departments that were decorated differently, each with a bit of its own personality, and under one roof you could find everything from electronics and music to clothes, appliances, and furniture. It was a one-stop shopping center, except it wasn't bland like Target and Walmart. The outdoor department at Two Guys was hilarious to my friends and me because they had everything you needed to go camping in the Catskills, but we lived in such an urban area that tents were as useful to us as space suits.

The most useless thing they had was a big orange canoe mounted on a wall, which sat there month after month. None of us had ever even seen a lake or a river, and no one brought a boat like that to the public pool.

One day, Louie, the older Luciano, coolly pointed to it and said, "I'm gonna steal the fucking canoe."

"No, you're not," I said. "How you gonna do that?"

"What do you mean?" he asked. He glared at us long enough that we realized he wasn't kidding. "Listen to me; it's a perfect crime. Why? Because nobody steals a fucking canoe."

We just nodded.

"Louie, if they see you taking it, they'll know you're stealing it," his brother said.

"No, no, no. Listen to me," Louie said. "I'm going to walk out like I just bought it. And no one is going to stop me, okay? Why would they? Are they going to think I stole the canoe? No way! They won't think that, because *no one steals a fucking canoe.*"

Off he went, casually, like he owned the joint. My father was like that too, because, like a lot of city people, he knew that if you act like you own the place, you can get away with anything. Unfortunately, computers and surveillance cameras have changed the odds on that quite a bit. These days the bar code that is your face is easy to track down, so if you walk out of a store with a canoe and don't set off an alarm, give them time, they will find you anyway. And when they do, if you've ever been caught with a joint or haven't paid a parking ticket, you'll probably end up doing three to five in Leavenworth.

Anyway, Louie strolled over and confidently removed the canoe from the wall without attracting any attention. Then he balanced it on his head and started walking calmly toward the door. We followed ten feet behind him, trying to be cool.

I need to tell you something about Louie. He was the first time I encountered "the pot-smoking laugh." I've encountered it many times since, but Louie was my first. The pot-smoking laugh is like a stutter, real low, almost a hiccup. It's just *ah-ha-ha-ha-ha*. It's uncontrollable, like marijuana-induced Tourette's. It's always in a weird tone that is drastically unlike the person's typical speaking voice. It's very common among heavy lifelong pot smokers, but it was a part of Louie's DNA by age fourteen. He was the Jeff Spicoli of Elizabeth, New Jersey.

The pot-smoking laugh is funny, but it's no joke, because if you cross that line, you'll never be the same. Just look at Sean Penn. He launched his acting career on that laugh and he's never been able to shake it. These days he gives speeches on world peace to the UN General Assembly and it sneaks up on him. I can imagine him there saying, "We can't let Castro pay these, *ah-ha-ha-ha-ha*." He can't help lapsing into Spicoli. The thing is, everyone ignores it because everything else he says is brilliant.

It's a slippery slope and it's hard to climb back up, so keep this in mind the next time you laugh while you're stoned.

What also happens with the pot-smoking laugh is that your head bobs up and down in time, making it even more obvious that you're a huge pot smoker. This takes the average person years, but Louie was there at fourteen. When he put the canoe on his head, he understandably started laughing, and because of his pot-smoking laugh, the canoe started bobbing up and down. The canoe also echoed and amplified his laugh, which freaked him out and made him laugh harder. He sounded like a madman in an asylum giggling at the end of a hallway: *ah-ha-ha-ha-ha!* But he didn't stop marching toward the door wearing the dumbest orange hat in the world.

Louie was right, by the way. It didn't matter how hard he laughed and bobbed on his way out—no one stopped him! The year was 1979, so there were no fancy alarm systems, just an old white guy who looked like Matlock if he had failed the bar exam. The guard actually paused as Louie approached, then nodded at him and told him to have a good weekend.

"Enjoy your weekend, son," the old guy said.

"All right, thanks, I will," Louie said. *"Ah-ha-ha-ha-ha!"* It was a very strange moment. It felt like the guard knew all about Louie's big plans to canoe down the nearest rushing river.

Louie was the coolest person I knew before stealing the canoe. Afterward he was a living legend. He was gambling before I knew what risking something even meant. Louie walked through the parking lot laughing so hard that he banged the canoe into every single car he passed as people cursed and jumped left and right to avoid him, and it was the greatest thing I'd ever seen.

Exactly twenty-four hours later, my buddy Mike called me. This is the how I remember the conversation.

"Are you sitting down?" Mike asked.

"Why? What happened?" I said.

"Listen to me, you have to sit down. You're going to laugh so hard."

"C'mon, man, what happened?"

"You didn't hear about Luciano, did you?"

"No."

"He got arrested."

"Why? He got busted for the canoe?"

"Yes! No! *Ah-ha-ha-ha-ha!* You sitting down?"

Louie Luciano made off with the canoe but the very next day got clipped at Two Guys for attempting to steal the oars! Somehow, that guard became Columbo overnight and bagged him.

"Hey!" the old guy said as Louie tried to slip out with the oars under his arm like two baguettes. "Hey, you there! Stop! Are you the guy who took the canoe?"

Apparently at that point, a younger guard tackled Louie, because Sherlock was in no shape for that.

Louie Luciano did time in juvie for his actions, by the way, and that was a terrible gamble on his part. He went to Boys Town because the canoe heist qualified as grand larceny. Grand larceny was being caught stealing goods with a value over $500, and the canoe's sticker price was $515. How about that crap luck? Stealing that boat was a grown-up crime in the eyes of the police by just $15.

If you saw a photo of me, hanging out with those guys, I wouldn't blame you if you predicted that I'd be dead by twenty-five (I would have bet the under myself). When Louie went off to juvie, that moment in time was gone for good, which is probably why some of us are still alive. After that summer, I lost track of the Lucianos and vice versa. Their parents were ne'er-do-well nomads who were never around to the degree that Tony lived with my girl-friend's family in high school for a while when things got really bad. My ex-girlfriend's father, who was a barber, was friends with the Lucianos' father. They referred to them-selves as *camparis*, which is Italian American slang for two friends whose families are intertwined all the way back to the old country. If you've got one, you can count on a *campari*.

Anyway, Louie was the king of the world in our neigh-borhood for twenty-four hours. He risked it all and won, then he got greedy and lost everything, all in the same day, which is how gambling works. It's a roller-coaster ride, and we all find different reasons to buy that ticket and buckle up.

Louie went back to the store because he needed the ac-cessories to sell the canoe. There was a guy in Newark who sold stolen goods out of a shop on North Seventh Street right by Branch Brook Park. He took it all: jewelry, radios, musical instruments, clothes, anything. Except canoes.

"What the fuck am I going to do with a canoe? This is fucking North Newark, kid. I can't sell a canoe."

Then he reconsidered. "Know what? I can sell it to my jerk-off cousin; he's outdoorsy. But I need the oars. Get me some oars, and you got a deal, kid."

The next day, Louie Luciano went back for the oars and ended up in Nebraska, in Boys Town, for six months. He came back even tougher, with a tattoo cut into his arm with a razor blade. It was a very creative prison tattoo—it said his name.

The thing that the Lucianos were best known for, by the way, was stealing car stereos. They made a killing doing it in the years following the canoe heist, up until the day they got caught. Tony, the younger brother, was better known as Sticky Elbows because every time he broke a window, the glass stuck to his arm. Every time.

The Lucianos were profiled by the cops and hauled into court before they were eighteen and were sentenced identically. They were given probation, and on their way out of court, they stole a pair of car stereos from the parking lot. They both made sure the cars that they stole from had government plates, hoping that one of them belonged to the judge who had just sentenced them.

Another kid I went to school with rode a bike out of the same department store. Same approach, same guard, same store. Like Louie, he figured that no one would question someone crazy enough to ride out on stolen wheels. There is a way to go so crazy with your plan that no one questions what you're doing. You confuse them so much that you're gone before they realize what just happened.

Expert gamblers and thieves of any age know how people think. They can predict the average person's reaction, and if there is one thing that the security guard at Two Guys Department Store was, it was average. That poor bastard was such a boob, probably a retired postman, who didn't expect the neighborhood youth to be so bold. But I have to give him credit; he momentarily got it together in those crucial twenty-four hours after the heist. He went home and came back at the top of his game, and was thereby able to apprehend Louie when he returned for the oars.

"Hey, you there!" the guard said eyeing the dead giveaway, the oars. "Stop! Are you the guy who took the canoe?"

2

LONG SHOT

At twenty-three, I had a job as a longshoreman working in Port Newark, and it was the first bit of stability that I experienced as a young man. Before I got the job, I spent a year working with my buddy in his family's machine shop, cleaning up. I'd oil the machines and sweep up the metal shavings, which invariably ended up as a thin layer of gray dust coating the top of the pizza we ate at the end of every shift. That job left me feeling even more hopeless and unsure of what I could possibly do with myself for the rest of my life. I had everything ahead of me and nothing in front of me with no idea whatsoever as to what was going to happen, until a different buddy's father, who was a major figure in the International Longshoremen's Association, took pity on our family situation and handed me a job at the port. My father's accident had ravaged our family; the medical bills, necessary home renovations, and equipment we needed to care for him at home left us in debt up to our ears. We were forced to go on welfare and live on food stamps, and for years we tried to get reimbursements from Medicaid but got next to nothing in the end. We needed a helping hand.

When I started the job, we were completely bankrupt. My mother is a very proud woman, so this upset her tremendously, but she'd had no choice. She had to take a second mortgage out on the house to pay for everything, and we were underwater trying to keep up with the payments, but between my new job and my mom's, we were able to keep the house and begin to get life back to normal.

I worked as a longshoreman for a year and a half, making $70,000, plus bonuses, which is a very good living when you're twenty-three years old and haven't graduated high school. But that wasn't enough for me, so in the fall of 1991, I gave my mother about $4,000 in spending money, plus another $5,000 that I'd put into a savings account (the first savings account I ever opened), and I told her that I wanted to quit my job and pursue a career in stand-up comedy. A few years earlier when I was nineteen, I'd tried stand-up twice, and both times I'd bombed. I've bombed a lot since and have seen countless people bomb, but I still count my first two stand-up attempts as some of the worst minutes of comedy I've ever seen.

Even though I lacked the balls to dust myself off and stick with it, I thought about it all the time. My jokes, which I continued to write, were passable, but that didn't matter, because I had a bigger issue: I wasn't comfortable onstage. Both times I'd frozen up like a deer in headlights and choked. Being onstage at a comedy club is disorienting because at most places, especially the rat holes where you can get time as a newcomer, the lights are in your face, so you know the audience is there, but you can't see most of them. You're up there, alone, under a microscope feeling the eagerness of an invisible group of people waiting to be entertained. It still fucks with my head sometimes.

I decided to take some acting classes, hoping to get comfortable performing in front of a crowd. That plan might have worked if I'd had the money to really commit to it, but I didn't, so I took one class in New York, and that was that. Instead of finding anything constructive to do with my free time, I spent my nights and weekends fucking around, hitting on chicks, drinking too much, and doing as much coke as I could afford. In my early twenties, cocaine replaced weed as my drug of choice, and I can trace that back to my job in the machine shop, because after sweeping up toxic dust all day and eating it like extra Parmesan on top of my dinner, all I wanted to do was get as high and drunk as possible before going back to do it all over again in the morning. I was living life day to day at best. When I got to the port, I made more money and the regimen helped stabilize things for me and for my family, but things were still pretty unstable. I was never going to be satisfied with my unfulfilled dream still eating at me, so the moment things leveled out, I asked my mother's permission to throw caution to the wind.

"Ma, this is going to sound corny, but there's no other way to put it," I said. "I have a dream in me. I can keep doing what I'm doing and we can both have a nice life, but I have a dream in me, and it's a big risk."

When I was in my twenties, being fifty held a lot of meaning to me. By fifty, I figured that I'd be old enough to wake up and hate myself for never trying comedy again and still young enough to have to live with my failure until the day I died. In my twenties, I thought that if I hadn't done it by fifty, I would rather be dead. I'm fifty now and have exceeded my dreams. I didn't expect to be as success- ful at comedy as I am; I never could have predicted getting on *Stern* or in any of the films or network TV shows that I've done. I would have been satisfied with a career on the road playing clubs, so long as I made a living. I knew in my twenties that by fifty, the resentment I'd feel for every- body doing what I'd wanted to do would be tremendous. If I never tried, I knew I'd hate them almost as much as I hate Aziz Ansari.

Resentment is a devil that will eat you up inside, which is why I tell the girls who date me that I absolutely have to cheat on them if I get the chance. Usually they don't fol- low my logic, but I'm not lying; if I have the chance to cheat and don't, I'll resent them forever! Take Dana, my ex-girlfriend, whom *Stern* listeners got to know very well during the five years that we dated. Things were casual between us until after the first time we took the show to Vegas for a week of live shows. When I returned, I asked Dana to be my girlfriend, which we talked about on the air, but the truth is that we were very much together be- fore I left. When I got back, though, I had a confession to make: I told her that I'd slept with a girl in Vegas, just once. The girl in question was a stripper–whore who I said came on to me, then charged me $500. That detail, as well as my confession, made it on to the air. I've never admitted this before because I didn't want to hurt Dana's feelings, but that wasn't true, and it also wasn't the end of the story.

We did the show live at the Hard Rock Hotel, outside by the pool, for five glorious days. In those five days, I didn't sleep with just one girl; I slept with eleven. Yes, that's right, *eleven*. Eleven *strippers* to be exact—and that tally includes two threesomes. Now that I'm being honest, they may have been stripper–whores, but I can't be certain, because I didn't pay for any of them. Most of them were employed by a major impresario who owns strip clubs with a name that sounds like Schmearmint Wino. I don't know if they were paid; I only know that they were seasoned pros.

At the time, Fred Norris was happily married with a beautiful new daughter, Howard was loyal to Beth, and Robin Quivers—being a sophisticated broadcaster and cultured person—had no interest in sordid pursuits. That left little old me to enjoy the spoils for the whole team! I felt like Elvis for five days and nights, and I loved every minute of it. In every casino, at every club, guys would chant my name, I had off–the–charts Vegas 12s hitting on me, all of them asking me to make them famous by mentioning their names and websites on the air. It was incredible. I was momentarily John Stamos, except funny.

For once in my life, I didn't need to tell a girl that I'd written *Jurassic Park* or that I was Newman from *Seinfeld* to get laid. No lie was better than the truth that I was on the biggest radio show of all time and that if I mentioned any stripper's or porn star's website on the air, the *Stern* audience would flock to them. All of them knew that *Stern* fans were exactly the kind of perverts who would pay for their live cams and buy their used panties and set them up for life. They also knew that I encouraged pay-for-play promotions, and I wasn't after cash.

"Do you have a website where you get guys off over the internet? Do you want to make a million bucks doing that? Let Uncle Artie help you out! Honey, I say your name on the airwaves and *whoosh*, your dream will come true! You see, Uncle Artie isn't on any old radio show, my little chickadee. He's not on your local yokel *Bob and Ted* morning drive, and he's not on the *Fuckaninny and Goofball Morning Madhouse*. He ain't on *Cousin Brucie* or the *Dicklick and Fruitloop Power Hour*. Uncle Artie is on the greatest radio show that ever was. He's on the one, the only *Howard Stern Show!*"

That year, in 2003, Arbitron, the wing of the Nielsen company that tracks radio ratings, did a study. By then, I had been on *Stern* for a couple of years, and I'm not saying it had anything to do with me, because I hopped on what was already a runaway gravy train. I will say that by '03, we were in a groove and, in my opinion, embarking on our best period together. The numbers reflected that, because according to Arbitron, in 2003, at 9:15 a.m. on the days when we did a live show, an average of fourteen million people were listening to us. *Fourteen million people!* I still can't believe that number. The population of the United States in 2003 was approximately 290 million, which means that at 9:15 a.m. on days when were live, roughly 5 percent of the entire population was listening. Considering what we were typically talking about, most of you should be ashamed of yourselves.

I loved to use that clout to my advantage and not just to get laid. Say I was playing Zanies in Chicago any given weekend—if I mentioned the gig on the air a few times, by Thursday it would be sold out. Living hell for a touring comedian is doing radio appearances in an unfamiliar town because his show isn't sold out. I never had to, which meant precious extra hours of sleep for me until the promoter picked me up at my hotel room thirty minutes before I had to go on. "Hey, buddy, come get me when it's time for me to put your kids through Harvard." Let's be honest: the promoter's kids were probably going to DeVry, but he could have afforded Harvard with all the tickets I sold. That's what the strength of fourteen million people can do.

Anyway, let's get back to the fact that I fucked eleven strippers in five days, which included two threesomes. I was the only guy in those threesomes, by the way, in case anyone is keeping the box score of this game. Box score—get it? I was in heaven; I was thirty-two years old, I had more testosterone coursing through my veins than José Canseco on juice, and for the first time in my life—for that week, at least—I experienced what it's like to be good-looking and desired by chicks. As I've already mentioned, when I got home, I told Dana that I'd slept with one stripper, and I took a gamble with how I chose to explain it.

"I had to, babe," I said. "I would have resented you if I didn't go through with it. I didn't seek it out or try to make it happen; it just fell into my lap. Every guy dreams of being a famous athlete or musician and having women throw themselves at their feet. My career has finally taken off to the point that in my world I'm a kind of rock star, so in certain situations, I can get laid because of that. I've wanted to experience that kind of treatment my entire life, but now I have you, and you're much more important. Sleeping with that one stripper was my way of making up for lost time. It was symbolic. I did it just the once, and I promise you, that's it."

Dana was easy to read, and I could tell that as mad as she was, she saw a small amount of truth in what I was saying, so I kept at it.

"Dana, I know this sounds crazy, but you have to understand that if I didn't do what I did, it would have become a big problem for us. When I looked back on my life and our relationship, I'd see you as the person who came between me and my one chance at fulfilling a rock star fantasy I've had since I was fourteen years old! And you know what would have happened? I'm not saying this is right, but I would have ended up resenting you for it."

"Really?" she asked. By this point, she looked more sad and concerned than angry.

"Really," I said. "I'd probably resent you for the rest of my life. And, honey, I don't want to do that."

Somehow she bought it. And in return, I bought her an Hermès handbag, so everyone went home happy. She got presents, and I got a steady date to industry parties. I'm just kidding. The truth is, Dana and I were very much in love for five years. She was my best friend and a great girlfriend, and of all the relationships I've had, I think Dana and I had what it took to have a great marriage and a life together if we'd been able to stick it out. We didn't stand a chance, because nothing can survive the combination of heroin and a life spent on the road. It still makes me sad to think about it. We were doomed by the only life I know how to live and the only gamble I regret taking.

For three years in a row, we did the *Stern Show* for one week in Vegas, each time at the Hard Rock Hotel, and each time Howard finagled a private jet through Viacom to fly us out. It was a fourteen-seat, G6 Gulfstream, with just six guys on board plus one smoking-hot stewardess. We'd drink, eat sushi, play poker; we'd fat-shame and body-judge and call women *chicks*. We talked about grabbing pussy and buying furniture, and if Billy Bush had come on board, he would have ended up skydiving home without a parachute.

In Vegas, the airport that services private jets is a stone's throw from the Hard Rock, so coming in to land, we'd get a bird's-eye view of the enormous pool, the stage, and the area they roped off for our show. There would be about four thousand strippers waiting there for us, hoping to get noticed and invited on the air. The first time I saw all those women in bikinis, I began shaking with anticipation. Honest to God, I had tremors and I said to myself, "This is it. This is almost what it must feel like to be a Rolling Stone."

I never would have experienced any of that, of course, if my mother hadn't allowed me to take that second swing at comedy. It was a gamble on both of our parts, and I'd say it paid off. I'll never forget the conversation. We were in our kitchen, and I told her what I wanted to do and that I'd put some money aside for her to live on. I said I'd get a job driving a cab to support myself so she wouldn't have to worry. She was quiet for a while, and I really had no idea what she was going to say.

"Art, I'll work two jobs if I have to," she finally said. "Just do it. Quit the port and try. But you have to really try. This is your last chance."

"Thank you, Ma. I promise you I will. Give me four

years. Consider it my college. Give me from twenty-two to twenty-six. If it doesn't work, if I can't make a living doing comedy in some way, I'll go back to the port and that will be the end of it."

Exactly three and a half years later, I was a cast member on *Mad TV*, and I've never looked back. I made about $300,000 that year, which was more money than anyone in our family had ever seen. I've managed to remain above that ever since, sometimes way above it and sometimes just squeaking by. I'm where I am because my mother took a chance. I also had a lot of luck. And I mean *a lot* of luck.

There's an old Italian phrase, it's either a Sicilian or Neapolitan dialect that an uncle of mine who is no longer with us used to say about me. He used to say it in Italian and explained that it translated to something like "idiot's luck." If you had it, you weren't aware of it, but it kept good things happening to you even though you were a fuckup. To him, that's what I was: a shithead who'd keep stepping in pots of gold my whole life, somehow blessed in a way that I didn't deserve. At holiday dinners and barbecues when he'd hear stories about stupid things I'd done, he'd just shake his head and say, "Yeah, he's gotta dat *ting*," and he'd point to the top of his head where I presume people like me have an invisible lucky halo hovering over them. Either that or he was indicating retardation.

Whatever it was, my uncle was right. There have been so many instances of "dat *ting*" saving my ass, but looking back on my life now, at fifty, I'm convinced that there's even more to it. I have to give myself some credit, because there's having "dat *ting*," but there's also knowing how to play it to your advantage. I've never felt that I could waltz through life leaving my fate up to Saint Cajetan, the Catholic saint of good fortune, and the patron saint of gamblers, but I have felt lucky in life. And this is where taking risks gets interesting, because if you ask me, luck is what you make of it. It's not a divine force beyond our control; it's an opportunity. It's like the benevolent older brother of risk looking out for you. But you may be stubborn, and you may ignore that older brother's advice. And if you do that, you're a loser who risked in vain and missed the boat.

Let me give you an example. Meeting my cowriter, Anthony, was all timing and luck. I would not have two bestselling books without him. I could have told the same stories the same way to another writer, but the resulting books wouldn't have been anything close to what they are. The fact that he was available at the time that I was ready to write a book was sheer chance, because he'd had a lot of success and had other offers on the table. He was also the first guy I met!

I remember my agent saying, "This kid Anthony wrote Slash's book, Eminem's book, and Tommy Lee's. See if you like him." I love Slash, I always have, so I bought the book in the airport on the way to a gig and I fucking devoured it during a week on the road. I literally could not put it down. I called my agent and said, "I want to meet this guy; I loved that book." The agent said, "Yeah, he's really good, and that's a great one; it got to number six on the *New York Times* Best Seller List. Don't get your hopes up, because you're not going to do that well, but I bet you'll make the lower end of the list, probably the top twenty at best because of Howard. I'll see if Anthony's interested." For many reasons, I later fired that agent, but after the book came out, it was so great to tell him, "Yeah, we made the top twenty, asshole; we made it all the way to number one."

I'm an avid reader and always have been, which might come as a surprise to my fans and haters alike. I'm always reading nonfiction, usually biographies and books about film, baseball, and American history. Writing a book had always been a dream of mine; I just never thought I'd find the guy for me. I'd met comedy writers, magazine writers, all kinds of writers who wanted to collaborate with me, but I hadn't met one that I wanted to spend more than an hour with, let alone spill my life story to. I didn't expect book writers to be any different. And the others I met weren't, but lo and behold, the first one I met was exactly my guy. I knew it right away, so I didn't deliberate. If I had, Anthony might have chosen another project and the words you're reading now might never had made it onto the page. In life, taking advantage of moments like that are just as important as taking the risks that define you. It's not only how much you bet, but for lack of a better cliché, it's also knowing when to hold 'em and when to fold 'em. Sure, I might have "dat *ting*," but for all my losses, I've heard luck when it's whispered in my ear. If you listen to your instincts and risk appropriately when the time is right, you'll end up exactly where you want to go. Learn to trust what your gut has to say, because it's the only thing that never lies to you.

3

SLIDING DOORS, PART I

Does anyone remember that Gwyneth Paltrow movie *Sliding Doors*? It came out in the late '90s, and it's about how different the main character's life would have been if she'd caught or missed a train on the way home from work. It's about parallel universes and possibilities and how one small detail can change everything. I've realized that the film speaks to the realities of my life quite a bit, not only because it's a dramatic rom-com but because a lot of people tell me that I remind them of Gwyneth Paltrow.

Timing has meant everything in my life and my career. Meeting Anthony and writing the books, meeting Norm Macdonald and being cast in *Dirty Work*, meeting Quincy Jones and landing a role on *Mad TV*—all these opportunities came to me as if they were waiting there just for me, and I pounced on them. But none of it would have meant a thing if my mother hadn't said, "Go for it." Quitting the port with her permission was the train I caught.

Now let's take a look at what my life would have been like if the subway doors had shut and I'd missed that uptown express. We have to rewind to 1991 and return to the Lange family kitchen, where my mother, Judy Lange, is having a different reaction to her only son's request to take another swing at his dream.

"Ma, I have a dream in me, I want to do stand-up comedy. I've made good money at the port the past year and a half, I've saved up a few grand here to give you to tide you over, and . . . well, I'd like to give it a shot."

In this version, my mother doesn't think it over very long. "Sorry, Art, you can't do that," she says. "We've been through hell and we are finally getting on our feet. You're making good money, and you need to keep it up. Forget about comedy. You tried it a few years ago and you were horrible."

I try to stay cool, but it isn't easy.

"You're funny, Art, you really are," she continues. "You make me laugh every day, but you're no comedian. Do you really think you're good enough to be on *David Letterman*? Who do you think you are? Some kind of Italian Seinfeld? Think about what happened last time. You have to keep your job. You've got a good thing going, and there's no way I can support us while you try to make it in comedy. I'm sorry."

"Okay, Ma. You're right. I love you. I'm going up to bed."

My mother, being a full-blooded Italian American, knows the power of maternal guilt. She knows that all Italian Americans respond to it. In reality, she would have had to say much less than she did in this fictional dramatization for me to have never thought of pursuing stand-up comedy

again. If she'd looked me in the eye a certain way and held
that stare long enough, that would have ended my ambitions
forever. Words would not have been necessary.

I would keep working at the port and never challenge
her decision. Something else would happen, though. That
night, a darkness would start gathering around me. At
first it would be just a storm on the horizon, off in the distance. It would grow more ominous over time, moving closer
as the years went by, until it was tailing me every waking
hour. When that tsunami of depression finally overtook
me, I would not have survived. Since my mother knows
me better than anyone in this world, maybe she saw that
future and decided that putting all her money on Artie to
place was better than watching her son run a race he
couldn't win.

But let's say she played it safe and I missed the train. I'm
fifty years old, so by now I would have been working as a
longshoreman at the port of Newark for thirty years. If I
hadn't gotten myself killed or arrested, I'd be making
really good money by now. I'd be happy that my mother
was well taken care of and enjoying a nice life, but I'd be
tortured by my unfulfilled dreams. The way I've usually
chosen to offset frustration in my life is by creating chaos
in order to distract me from my own unhappiness. If I
were still a longshoreman at fifty, there is no doubt that
my life would be complete chaos, because it was already in
motion when I left. I'd been given a plum lifelong job that
required very little of me to keep it, so what did I do? I
got embroiled in a few of the small handful of things that
would have gotten me fired, if not worse.

The International Longshoremen's Association is defined

by connections and family ties. You don't get a job by strolling in, dropping off your résumé detailing your experience as a barista, and explaining to the head of HR that you're looking for a new challenge. You need to know a guy or a guy who knows a guy. My friend's father, who we will call Mr. DiStefano, vouched for me; he even got me hired at a better wage than an average first-year union joe. He was a major player in the union and he looked after me, even telling people that I was a second cousin. That went a very long way, as you'll soon see. He was supportive and kind, but he wasn't Mother Teresa. The guy was very unapproachable and very intimidating. To become powerful in a union like that, you cannot be a cupcake, so basically every millennial in America would find his management style unacceptable.

When I was around him, I was never sure if he liked me or wanted to break my arm. Before my first day, I met him in his office, and he told me that he would watch out for me and that if I got into any trouble I should let people know that he was the one who got me the job. This was huge, because he was basically granting me protection, the way a Mafia godfather did to those who needed it in the neighborhood.

"What kind of trouble do you mean, Mr. DiStefano?" I asked.

"Gambling, stealing, importing drugs. People will try to drag you into it. Anyone tries to do that with you, let me know. I don't care what you do when you're not on the job. You can sell drugs, steal cars, I don't give a fuck what you do. But you get involved with anything down here? We've got beef. You understand?"

"Yes, I do."

By the way, if you don't know anything about the long-shoremen, do yourself a favor and watch *On the Waterfront*, starring Marlon Brando, one of the greatest films of the twentieth century. Once you've seen it, you'll understand a lot about this period of my life.

Mr. DiStefano was head of the International Long-shoremen's Association, which was a huge achievement, because he wasn't of Italian or Irish descent. No one other than Italians or Irishmen had held the position for decades, but he worked his way through the stranglehold the two ethnic groups had on those coveted union positions and got himself elected. He's a tough motherfucker who could both lead a mob of workers and play the political game. He's also currently under house arrest, by the way, but for the record, I never saw him do anything illegal.

Hey, if you think our presidential elections are rigged, especially this last one, you haven't seen shit. When you're in the union, the head of your crew tells you who to vote for on Election Day, literally standing over you as you do it. I admire that. To me, it's a more honest method of being crooked.

Anyway, everyone at the pier where I started working knew "who I was with," and I couldn't have been more set up. That's how they talk about connections down there— they talk about "who you're with." I was new, with no family members already working there like most guys, but I had some juice. And the perks of the job were not to be believed! We broke for lunch at noon and weren't expected back until 1:30. Now that's a union! With an hour and a half to dine, we'd go to Down Neck, which is also known as the Ironbound section of Newark, and we'd feast like kings. There is a diversity of incredible restaurants there serving the ethnic groups that have established themselves in Jersey over the years. There is Portuguese, Spanish, and Italian food, and places that combine all three into a style you won't find anywhere else. You can get paella, zuppa di pesce, cuts of steak cooked all different ways—you can find whatever you want. There's a place called Tony Da Caneca that I love and the Spanish Tavern, which has the most amazing bread. One of my favorites was a Cuban place run by a guy who claimed that Tupac Shakur was alive and well and living in Cuba. He was very convincing, claiming that he'd shared a cigar with him and been to a party at his house. This made no sense at all, because Tupac hadn't been murdered yet.

There is an ice cream place called Nasto's that we'd go to afterward, which was like this Willy Wonka factory in the middle of all these great restaurants. Except it was Newark, so Willy Wonka would have had to be more like a wiseguy. In his factories, the schnozzberries don't taste like schnozzberries; they taste like gabagool. The movie based on him wouldn't be *Willy Wonka and the Chocolate Factory*; it would be *Uncle Frankie and the Gabagool Factory*, because in Uncle Frankie's factory, you fat fucks, everything tastes like gabagool! In his factory, the Oompa-Loompas aren't orange; they're red, white, and green! See how much fun writing books can be? Hemingway didn't have this much fun writing *A Moveable Feast*.

SO FOR A YEAR and a half, I worked on the orange juice pier unloading gallons of orange juice with a bunch of guys I got to know pretty well. The one thing that brought us all together no matter how different we were was that we would get a bonus at the end of the year based on how many ships we unloaded. It was an incentive to work as a team, and we did that really well. We made the bonus that year and each walked away with a few thousand dollars, which I gave to my mom.

Then they changed our crew and broke up the winning team. I got reassigned to another pier, which also unloaded orange juice. This one, however, was owned by a different guy who took a very different approach to labor policy. The day I started was the day the owner decided to break the union by hiring a bunch of South Americans willing to work fifteen hours a day for nine dollars an hour. I couldn't blame him, because the guys in our crew were getting forty dollars an hour and spent most of the day playing 500 Rummy on the job.

The scabs he hired were Portuguese-speaking South Americans that he bused in on former prison buses with bars over the windows. Good thing he did, because the longshoremen tried to kill them every single day the strike lasted. I refer again to *On the Waterfront* when I say that longshoremen don't strike—they riot. There's no peaceful picket lines or organized demonstration; there's violence and shouting. The cops usually let it run its course, because many of their brothers and fathers are longshoremen. When those poor scabs showed up, they were greeted with rocks, bottles, and Molotov cocktails on the way in and on the way out, every single day. Welcome to the port, scabs! As a longshoreman assigned to that pier, I was expected to join in and try to beat the shit out of any scab I got my hands on.

As much as I was all for the union, I didn't want any part of it. I didn't want to kill some poor guy who probably sent his nine bucks an hour back home to his family in South America. The whole thing was brutal. I saw a guy tear his own brother out of a truck and beat him with a lead pipe because he was driving some scabs to work. So I skated by doing the minimum every day. I'd show up and yell a lot, and move around in the crowd, but really spent most of my time on the outskirts of the fight with a six-pack. To fit in, occasionally I'd throw an empty Bud long-neck at a bus. This was the same week that I told my mother I wanted to try comedy again and the end of my time in the union.

But if I'd missed my train and she'd told me to keep working, I wouldn't have left. I would have stayed striking until it was settled and we went back to work. And at my new job, I would have already fucked up my future, because, despite the strict warning from my mentor, before lunch on my first day at the new pier, I'd already gotten into trouble.

Some guy introduced himself and pulled me aside. "Hey. Take this bag to this Cuban deli in Elizabeth. You know where that is?"

"Yeah," I said. "But why should I do that?"

"Just take the bag. If everything is in order, the guy will give you a hundred. And when you come back, I'll give you another hundred."

"So I deliver a bag and get two hundred bucks?"

"Yeah, that's right," he said. "It's easy. He gives you a C-note, I give you a C-note. And you make two hundred bucks at lunch."

I knew this was exactly what Mr. DiStefano had warned me about, but you see, I'd already broken his code during my time at the other pier. Betting on sports is a big thing down there, and since it's something I really enjoyed, I'd gotten into it pretty heavily. During a busy week with a lot of traffic, I'd make about $1,200, which was plenty— unless you owed money to a shylock. You never want to borrow money from a shylock, because the interest is worse than those credit cards they use to lure unsuspecting college freshmen into a lifetime of debt. But I had to do it because I'd lost a few big bets with a bookie and the guy had to be paid if I wanted to keep my legs.

I borrowed enough money from the shylock to pay off the bookie, and I had my job and a steady paycheck, so in time, both he and I knew that I'd be able to pay him off— at a huge loss, of course. The amount wasn't enough to put me under, so I was all right, and I felt even better about the situation, because I had left that pier. It felt like the temptation was gone and I'd gotten a new start. Until I decided to become a bagman before lunch on my very first day. A bagman is the courier who carries money between a bookie and the guys that place their bets with him week in and week out. It is a highly illegal occupation.

I drove to Elizabeth that day, followed the owner of the Cuban deli into a back room, gave him the bag, and saw that it was full of cash. It was full of exactly eighteen grand, which I know because he counted it in front of me. At the time, I'd never seen that much money in one place, most of it crisp, clean hundred-dollar bills.

"Good," he said and nodded at me. "All here." He peeled off one of those new hundreds and handed it to me.

I drove back, returned the empty bag, and was told by the first guy that the Cuban guy had called and that everything was in order. He handed me my second hundred.

"So tomorrow," the guy said, "we do the same thing. You mind doing this every day? A different deli? You'll know the route in no time."

Correct me if I'm wrong, but does anyone know any happily retired bagmen? As far as I know, every bagman ends up dead or in jail. That was my future, because this guy thought he had me hooked. Actually, he did have me hooked, because he had something on me, which put me in his pocket for good. Compared to my father and some of the kids I grew up with, I don't have very many street smarts, but even I knew that this was a fucked-up situation.

"Listen," I said to the guy, "can I ask you a question?"

"Yeah, go ahead."

"What would happen if all eighteen grand wasn't there? Let's say I drive over tomorrow and there happens to be seventeen grand? I'm not saying how that might happen, but let's say it does. Who gets blamed for that, me or you?"

"What do you think?" he said.

"What do I think? I think I take the blame, and I think you're an asshole. I ain't risking that every day. Not for two hundred bucks, not for anything."

"What's wrong with you?" he said. "Don't be so uptight; today went fine."

"Yeah, sure it did. Today was fine, but that's the bait. There's a lot that can go wrong here, and I'll be the one taking the hit when it does."

"Nah, c'mon, all the guys that work here are honest guys," he said. "They'd never do that to me or to you! C'mon, don't be a jerk-off." Then he stared at me for a second. "Who you with, anyway?"

I told him the name.

"Bullshit," he said. "No way."

"Check it out. I'm not lying to ya. I'll see ya later."

The next morning, before breakfast, the guy found me and started enthusiastically kissing my ass.

"Hey, I have to apologize," he said. "I'll never ask you to run a bag for me again. I had no idea. Please tell Mr. DiStefano that I'd never do that to someone in his family. I made a big mistake."

I found out later that Mr. DiStefano also hated the guy running bags, so he sent a stronger message than usual that I was protected. I was never fucked with again, but if I wasn't with Mr. DiStefano, I would have been fucked. That day I learned that I was surrounded by dangerous people. If they tried to turn me out as a bagman on my very first day, what the hell would they do by the end of the week? These guys were dirtier than my last crew; they were everyday bagmen, which means they were involved in a real racket that probably extended beyond betting. God knows what the owners of those delis were moving, because there was no end to the illegal activities at the port. The DEA regularly seized boxes that were welded onto the bottoms of boats, full of kilos of blow. Merchandise from cars to electronics routinely disappeared, because if it was shady, it was going down at the port.

What I did that one day could have meant ten years behind bars. There was eighteen grand in that bag, and if you're moving anything over ten, you're in real trouble. I also went from county to county with it within the state, which carries more penalties. But because my friend's father got me the job and vouched for me, I was in the clear. Instead I got a grade-A apology.

And later that week, after my mother gave me the vote of confidence, I took two days to get up the courage to tell Mr. DiStefano that I was leaving. I was terrified that he would take my decision personally, but he didn't. He asked me to stay on another week so he could find a replacement, and that was that.

"Good luck, Art," he said. "Do your best. If it doesn't work out, I'll see you back here in six months. I'll have a job for you."

"I can't thank you enough for that; I hope I won't need it," I said.

"Listen to me," he said, staring me down across his desk. "What your mother went through with your father and not being able to get any money back from the insurance, all of that was horrible. She almost died taking care of him while raising you and your sister. Your family was on welfare; that was hard for you. Your mother still has a big mortgage on the house. You've got a job for seventy grand, right now, which you won't have if you leave. I have to ask you, why do you want to struggle again?"

"It's just something I have to do."

He kept staring at me for what seemed like an eternity. Sitting there in his office, my plan didn't make much sense to me either.

"Well, okay, Artie."

The guys in my former crew didn't help matters much. They thought I was the biggest idiot they'd ever met.

"*You* think you're gonna make it in *show business*?"

"So you're going to act? Like what, an idiot?" Their jokes would be followed by at least three minutes of laughter.

They weren't wrong, because what were the odds? I tried not to doubt myself, but it wasn't easy, and I felt like a selfish prick, but I knew I had to do it. It's hard to explain how I knew it was right, but it was like a voice inside telling me to. Outwardly, I felt like I was spitting in my mother's face, because things had gotten back to normal and I was turning it all upside down again. But I went for it, because I had to.

My sister, on the other hand, had found her way into a stable life, because she'd left the house earlier than I had, even though she felt guilty about doing so. She was not there the morning my father died and that bothered her for a long time, even though she was very close by, in Hoboken. I needed to live at home and help my mother because I was the fuckup who didn't go to college. My sister was never that, and she should never feel guilty about having her shit together. Staying home and helping however I could was my only way of giving back.

My dad did have one worry about my sister, but I was able to handle that situation for him. This is the exact conversation my sister, Stacey, and I had when it seemed to me that she and her boyfriend were getting serious.

"Stacey, you've got to leave that guy. You can't marry him," I said.

"Why would you say that? What's wrong with him?"

"He sells cocaine, and you shouldn't be with a guy who sells cocaine."

"You don't know what you're talking about," she said. "How do you know he sells cocaine?"

"Because I've bought cocaine from him."

"Fuck you, Artie!"

She punched me in the face, stormed out of the room, and was upset with me for a quite a while. But in the end, she didn't marry him, so mission accomplished, Dad.

I must take a moment to salute my sister for her strength and what she made of herself during the hardest time our family has ever known. Our father became a quadriplegic between her junior and senior years of high school, which is supposed to be the best time of your life. Stacey still got straight As and was accepted to Rutgers University. We had no money, but she got in and she went. She hated it, though, and didn't want to be there. She wanted to be in the city and go to more of a tech school, so she applied to FIT, got in, and paid her way by bartending the entire time. She is so much stronger than I'll ever be. She didn't need drugs or drinking to cope; she threw herself into achievement. She incurred student loans and has paid them all off herself. Right out of college she got a job with Phillips-Van Heusen, then after just six months got a job at Polo designing for Ralph Lauren. Then she jumped to Abercrombie & Fitch, then back to Polo because they begged her to return. Two years later, American Eagle offered her a big move. She wrote her ticket and got all she wanted and was there for fourteen years, heading up the entire men's design department.

One day not too long ago, I said to my ma, "You know, you should feel good. I know you think you did something wrong raising us, because I know I've been a handful, but you didn't, because we've both made something of ourselves." At the time, we were watching *The Howard Stern Show* on the E! Channel. "Mom, look, you should be proud of this!" There I was cohosting next to Howard, who happened to be wearing a shirt that my sister had designed. I said, "Clearly you did something right!" My sister and I have seen the world thanks to our jobs: she's been all over Europe and Asia, and I went to Afghanistan to entertain the troops. Our mom should be nothing but proud. She should be prouder of Stacey, of course, because she's a strong, respectable person in every way. Let's face it: aside from my job, I'm a complete loser.

4

SLIDING DOORS, PART 2

Excuse the pun, but I got a little derailed there, so allow me to continue with what would have happened if I'd missed that train. My mentor got me out of trouble that time, but I'd put good money on me diving headfirst into being a bagman. I think I would have used his influence for exactly what he didn't intend me to use it for—to get into, not out of, trouble. I would have gone back to the guy who recruited me to be a bagman and told him that I wanted in and that he'd better never ever fuck me over. I would have used Mr. DiStefano as my insurance policy, instead of my get–out–of–jail–free card because what could be more of a gamble than that!

I would have convinced myself that I needed that side gig, because I had a shylock to pay off. But running bags wouldn't have really been about paying off my debt; it would have been about increasing the danger in my life. Running bags would have been exciting! Life must be thrilling for me to want to live it, and when it's not, I find a way to make it so. It's too bad that I don't enjoy the rush of exciting, legal activities like bungee jumping, because I chase the same adrenaline high. The difference is that I get mine by doing what I'm not supposed to do instead of jumping off a bridge with a giant rubber band tied to my leg. Gambling is my skydiving, and let me tell you, when you gamble with money you don't have, the free fall lasts forever.

Anyway, that's how it would go. I'd do everything I wasn't supposed to at work, and it all would have gotten worse as time went on. With each passing year, I'd see the inevitable path of my life as a longshoreman, so I'd need to find a way to kick it up a notch. Eventually it would all blow up in my face and I'd either have beef with Mr. DiStefano or be roughed up by a bookie, a shylock, or a coworker—maybe all three. Being involved in a gambling ring, I would have exposed my mother and sister to a world where they could be physically and financially hurt because of my actions. I wouldn't have my dream, but I'd have more chaos than I knew what to do with. Eventually I'd be fired from the union and unable to work at the port after making an enemy of Mr. DiStefano. Instead of sitting here talking about this alternate universe years later, within a year, I would have been incarcerated.

In this version of my life, jail is unavoidable. So I do my time and I get out. Or I never get out. When coming up with probable scenarios, it's best to look at similar case studies, so here's one: I had a buddy in high school who did a crime, got caught, and went to Rahway State Prison, which is where I would have ended up if I'd gotten caught running bags in New Jersey. This kid, not much of a brain surgeon, robbed a gas station with a water pistol and went to jail when we were in our early twenties.

Let's use his life as an indication of what would have been in store for me in prison. He got raped by a guy in the shower, got AIDS because of it, and died behind bars. That's what happened to my buddy from biology class, and I can't think of a darker way to go: dying of full-blown AIDS in a prison hospital at twenty-five. By the way, he robbed that gas station with a metallic-blue water pistol that he won in Seaside Heights after he knocked down a few milk bottles at one of the stands on the boardwalk. He painted it black to look like a real gun. He was a tough kid in high school too; nobody fucked with him. He went from that to being somebody's girlfriend in prison. He used to call our one friend crying, telling him what was going on. I can't think of anything anyone could possibly say to comfort someone in that situation.

I like to remind myself of this when I catch myself complaining too much while going about my business. This might come as a surprise, but sometimes I complain. Sometimes I get up from an afternoon nap in my beautiful apartment, look out at my view of Manhattan, and realize that I have to drive to a gig, in traffic, so that I can say ridiculous things into a microphone and get paid for it. I'll leave for that gig knowing that usually I receive between thirty and fifty grand for my efforts, and still I'll complain about the traffic. If there happens to be traffic on the way home, I'll complain about it then too. I don't know about you, but sitting in all that traffic gets me depressed, even with a check for thirty to fifty grand in my pocket. Some days when I wake from my nap, knowing about the traffic I'll sit in, I find it hard to even get in the shower. It is one hell of a cross to bear.

What snaps me out of it is knowing how I'd feel if I'd missed my train. I'd be waking up every day in Rahway State Prison instead of my apartment, knowing full well that there would be no traffic delays when my prison boyfriend decided to fuck me. The best scenario that I'd hope for every morning is that he'd fuck my asshole. When you're a prison girlfriend, you don't get to choose where your boyfriend fucks you. Best case, your asshole; worst case, your mouth. Actually, the worst case is if he fucks both, and God help you if he fucks your asshole first. I'm getting lost in the details here; my point is that some version of this would be my life every single day. How about that for an alternate reality? It certainly would have brought a sense of structure to my life, which my high school guidance counselor told me I lacked, though I don't think this is the type of structure he had in mind. So in prison, in my twenties, I'd at least know what every day had in store for me. The only change I could expect in this version of my life would come if my boyfriend tired of me and decided to trade me for a pack of Newports. That would be an exciting time of transition . . . until my new boyfriend decided how he'd fuck me every day. That was my friend's life, and it could have been mine.

Risk is a fascinating thing. It's seductive and necessary, it can bring you everything or take all that you've got. We all take risks, the only difference being the degree. If my mother didn't take a chance on me, my life wouldn't have been very funny. I'd still be a wiseass, of course, but I'd also have a gaping ass. Instead of living in a penthouse, I'd live in a cell. Instead of a girlfriend with big tits, I'd have a boyfriend with big tits. Instead of sending my hot girl-friend out for a pack of cigarettes, I'd get sold as a girlfriend for a pack of cigarettes. Instead of never seeing or hearing my girlfriend shit, I'd do nothing but see and hear my boyfriend shit. Instead of having a girlfriend who is about twenty-five in my life, I'd be someone's girlfriend for about twenty-five to life.

5

THE BAD COP

One of my oldest living friends is a guy named Dan Mc-Grath, who fans of the *Stern Show* know as "the Bad Cop." Since we're talking about risks and luck, probability and possibility, and betting with both your money and your life, we have to talk about Danny. This guy has been a world-class risk-taker since I first met him. He also happens to be someone who hasn't won most of his life's bigger bets. Actually, now that I think about it, he hasn't won any of his life's bigger bets, and that has made all the difference.

I did a stand-up gig in late 2015, at the Stress Factory in New Brunswick, New Jersey, and Danny came to see me. He was seated in the front row, which I didn't realize until I got onstage. It threw me off, because I tell comedy club owners never to put somebody from my guest list anywhere near the front where I can see them. It's not because I don't appreciate them being there or because I don't think they deserve a good seat; it's because I find their presence distracting if I'm made aware of it. Dan was on my guest list, of course, because he couldn't afford a ticket, and he looked so awful because he abuses drugs and doesn't bathe that the owner figured that his name had to be a mistake. He didn't think that Dan could possibly be one of my guests, so he decided to seat this strange homeless-looking guy in the front to give me someone to goof on. Before I continue, I need to give you some background on Dan so that you fully appreciate this story.

Dan has struggled with drugs for most of his life, which is something I also know a lot about. But unlike me, Dan never found financial security, so he's had no way to support himself, let alone cover up the damage his habit has done to him. For example, a few years ago, Dan literally had about five or six teeth left in his mouth because the rest had rotted and fallen out. Never take oral hygiene for granted, because you can die from neglecting your teeth to that degree by poisoning your own blood. Dan's mouth was in such a sorry state that I did what any good friend would do and paid for him to see a dentist and get a new set of teeth. He was very excited about this and, frankly, so was I. Finally I could buy him a meal in public without him scaring the appetite out of everyone else in the restaurant. He called it "chewing solid food again." I called it "progress."

The very next day, I called Danny at work to see how he liked having teeth. His boss told me that he never showed up that morning, which surprised me, so I started calling his cell phone. He didn't pick up, so I left messages.

"Oh, hi, Dan. I see you didn't go to work today. What are you doing, walking around, smiling?" That was one.

"Dan, it's Artie. Hey, are you out there in the world eating frozen Kit Kats, walking around like a big shot?" That was another.

"Hey, Dan, Artie again. I hear you didn't go to work and you're not picking up, so I'm guessing that you're too busy doing all the things in life for which teeth are required."

"Dan, it's Artie. Your boss called me, he told me you went out bobbing for apples. I bet you caught more than last time!"

I didn't hear from Dan for three days. I'll let you fill in the blanks about what he was doing. Need a hint? It rhymes with *whack*.

When I took the stage at the Stress Factory that night in 2015, I saw Danny right away, because he's hard to miss, and on the spot, I ditched the bit I intended to open with and told the following story about him instead. He and I both graduated Union High School in 1985 but didn't see each other much over the summer. I had no idea what Dan had planned for the fall, but I wondered, because after all, I didn't have any plans myself. I finally ran into him on a Sunday night in the first week of September in the game room at Union County College, which is where my friends and I used to go to try to hustle people at pool. We'd shoot nine-ball and try to make beer money off drunk college kids and whoever else would play us.

From what I gathered, when Dan wasn't going to high school parties, hustling pool in the game room and the pool halls around town was what he'd done with his summer. He talked about it seriously, as if it were his summer job. Neither of us had harbored ambitions of getting into an Ivy League institution, but believe it or not, I recall the two of us tossing around the idea of going to a state or county school while standing around a keg at a party senior year. Union County College, where we liked playing pool, was a very viable option for us. Back then, it cost about $400 a semester if you were a resident of the county and had a pulse.

"Danny, what are you doing this fall?" I asked him. "Are you going to school here at County?"

"I'm either going to County or I'm taking the cop exam," he said, lining up his next shot.

"The cop exam. Do you want to be a cop?"

"No, not really."

"But you're thinking of taking the test."

"Yeah, I'll take the test if I don't enroll in college."

I was very confused. "Dan, fall semester starts next week, doesn't it?" I asked. "There is a deadline for enrolling in classes."

"Yeah, I know."

"So how do you not know if you're going or not?" I said, and I laughed a little bit. "I mean, it's just around the corner. Wouldn't you know by now?"

"Listen, man," he said, walking the length of the table, full of confidence. "If the Giants cover tonight, I'm going to Union County." He looked at me a minute before lining up his shot. "That's all I know."

I could tell he wasn't kidding, but I didn't know how he could be serious.

"Dan, wait a minute," I said. "What are you talking about? I'm as big a fan as you are, man, but what do the Giants have to do with your college career?"

"Here's the deal, Art. My parents gave me enough money for the first semester, and they told me to register here. I told them I registered, but I haven't done it yet, because I'm not sure I want to go. So I bet all the money on the Giants game tonight. If they cover, I go to school and I go in style. If they don't cover, I don't go to school. The decision will be made for me, and I'll take the cop exam."

I'm not kidding; this really happened. One of my best friends put his future in the hands of the New York Giants, which, as much as I love them, is a dicey proposition even in their good years.

"Dan, if you're serious, which I think you are," I said, "let's get out of here and watch the fucking game, man. It's about to start!"

I called all our friends from a sports bar nearby and told them to meet us because for the next three hours we were going to watch Dan McGrath's future unfold. A few showed up, but most of them thought I was pulling their chain. The next three hours were exciting, but to put it lightly, it wasn't the best night for Big Blue.

I shared this story with the crowd at the Stress Factory that night in 2015, never revealing that Dan was in the room, right there in the front row. Some time had passed since I'd bought Dan his new teeth, and it was as clear to me, even from the stage, that he hadn't followed the brushing and flossing regimen recommended by his dentist. Those pearly whites, his second set, had gone brown and begun to fall out. He looked like a toothless hobo, worse than ever, with dark concentric circles all the way around his eyes. He was also painfully thin, like an Olsen twin on a hunger strike.

I kept glancing at him while I told the story, but never long enough to make it obvious that I was talking about him. I tried to watch his reaction in my peripheral vision, because the story was killing. Who wouldn't laugh at a guy who gambled his future on an early-season Giants game? I let the laughs peter out, which took at least a full minute and a half.

"Everybody . . . guess what?" I said. "Dan, that same Dan, is here tonight."

Laughs immediately and a few people saying, "Noooo!"

"Yes, he is. He's here, I swear to God. He's in this very room, and I am not kidding."

I paused. I looked at them.

"I'm going to introduce you. Stand up, Dan," I said, pointing at him.

Dan stood up, slowly.

"Here he is. Don't be shy, Dan. Turn around. Let everyone get a good look at you."

Dan kind of smiled, which was gruesome, then turned around.

"So, guys," I said, "what do you think? Did the Giants cover?"

I love this story because it is as strong a cautionary tale as I've ever heard. The moral of it is as clear and obvious as a fairy tale. Danny *literally* gambled with his life; he bet all his potential and possibilities and left it up to chance. And he lost! Dan wasn't even an NFL stat aficionado, so it's safe to say that he made a knee-jerk bet and that decision changed the course of his life.

You might think that losing your shot at a college education over a Giants game would be a sign to change your ways or at least question your instincts. Not to Dan. He's what I like to call a pure-hearted gambler, the kind who loves the chase and never learns. He didn't change at all. He did, however, take the cop exam, and went on to an infamous career in law enforcement until he was dishonorably discharged ten years later. He and his girlfriend even got mixed up with some coke dealers, and when her father found out, he went right to Danny's superiors and that was the end of the line for him.

Danny had broken the law, but he didn't do time because nothing he'd done was that bad in the bigger scheme of things. Cops know that if a cop goes to jail, it's basically a death sentence. You've got a cement fortress full of criminals and the new blood is a cop. Gee, I wonder what's going to happen? In Dan's case, he'd put a lot of dealers away, so he had plenty of enemies on the inside. If you ask me, a cop heading to jail should be given a revolver and one bullet so he can do the right thing because he won't last a single night in the big house. Thank God they made Danny a civilian again, put him on probation, and let him go without pension or a recommendation of any kind. It was merciful, but in every other respect he was completely fucked. Good luck getting a job after you're dishonorably discharged from the police force. Nobody will hire you. Basically you end up begging for dishwashing shifts at Macaroni Grill.

I lived in Los Angeles for six years, from 1995 to 2001, which is when Danny's life took a swan dive into the gutter, so I witnessed this tragedy from afar. When I left, he was a cop, he was in great shape, and he'd always been good-looking, so factor in the uniform and it's safe to say that he was doing well with the broads. Danny always got lots of pussy when we were growing up, so as a cop, he was a rock star. He was making cop money, which isn't great by any means, but when you're twenty-three, it's enough to have a fucking ball. Last I saw him before I moved, he was living with this really hot Filipino chick whose father was a doctor. She had money and a nice condo, and life was looking good for Dan. When I spoke to him on the phone, he made it seem like everything was cool, even though it sounded to me like he was having more fun than cops were supposed to. Cops are no angels, but I could tell he was taking it too far. But who was I to judge? There I was on the other side of the country, drinking too much Jack Daniel's and doing too much blow and undermining my career in TV by constantly pushing the boundaries.

If you're reading this and don't know anything of my inglorious past, I'll keep it short and sweet by saying that once I got what I always wanted, which was a paying career in show business, I fucked it all up. I was a cast member on a sketch comedy show produced by the one and only Quincy Jones and was really excelling there, which I responded to by putting it all at risk. And I went down in flames; at the end of a long coke bender that lasted several days, I ran off set, made a scene in a grocery store, and ended up punching a cop in the face, while still in possession of a huge bag of coke. I was arrested, charged, and immediately released from the show. If you haven't heard that cute little bedtime story before, you'll find it told in great detail in *Too Fat to Fish*.

I still think what I did—and I punched a police officer—

pales in comparison to Danny's self-sabotage. After blowing his shot at college on a Giants game, he became a coke-addled cop, and then upped the ante by becoming a runner for a bookie while still on the force! Now that I think of it, that's another reason I would have ended up as a pawn in an illegal gambling operation if I'd continued life as a longshoreman—because Danny was already doing it. A runner is a cut above a bagman, by the way; he's the bookie's messenger who takes bets and visits regulars every week. When you're a runner, you're trusted and a part of the machine. Even in our most corrupt states, however, a member of law enforcement cannot be a runner for a bookie; it's more legal and acceptable to sodomize your cousin. It would have been stupid enough if Danny did this when he was off duty, but he didn't. He did it *while on duty as a cop.* That meant he'd show up in his cop car, wearing his cop uniform, to collect bets or deliver money. He had turned his life into a Scorsese movie.

When I would come home to visit my family during those six years, I'd place bets with Danny, as much as I couldn't fucking believe what he was doing. At the time, my mom lived about fifty miles away from where we grew up, but Danny drove down there anyway in his squad car, each time with a different rookie partner. That kid would be nervous as hell, even more so because Danny would keep telling him to shut up and not tell anybody. One time, we were in my mom's driveway when the cop radio in their cruiser went off. The dispatcher on the other end requested that all available cars respond immediately to an incident. Danny had no intention of doing that and actually looked annoyed as he leaned over and shut the radio off.

"Dan, what are you doing?" I asked him. "You've got to at least try to show up for that."

"Don't worry about it; they'll get it," he said.

"What do you mean, 'they'll get it'?"

"There's guys closer than us; they'll get it."

"Yeah, but, Dan, suppose that happened and you were the closest car? What then?"

"It wouldn't matter; they'd get it. There's enough of us to go around."

As funny as I thought it was, I could not believe what I was hearing.

"Dan," I said. "Listen to me. If Internal Affairs assigned a guy with severe Down syndrome to your case, you know what would happen?"

"What?"

"That guy would bust you. Dan, the way you're behaving, a deaf, dumb, and blind Internal Affairs investigator could catch you. What the hell are you doing?"

"You've got it all wrong, Art. Everything is under control."

On the days that Dan did shifts as desk sergeant, he treated manning the front desk at the station as if he were working the phones in a bookie's back room somewhere in Staten Island. He would leave real calls, probably emergencies, on hold while he took bets from his boss's clients. And if you've ever seen a cop show, then you're probably aware that every single call that comes into a police station is recorded, because that's the law. That didn't bother Dan one bit, because he'd thought of everything. One day when he was on a desk shift, he called me to shoot the shit, and as we were talking, he started to ask me if I wanted to place bets that week.

"Dan, what's wrong with you? You're at work. I'm not putting in a bet on the cop phone!" I said. Right after I said it, we heard a loud beep, which is what happens when you call the police; there is a beep every ten seconds to remind you that you're being recorded.

"I know, I know," he said, "but don't worry about it. I've got a system."

Beep.

"Are you serious, Dan? No, you don't. This is a cop phone, and we're being recorded."

Beep.

"I've got a system. Listen to me. A lot of teams are animals, like the Lions and the Dolphins, and everybody likes animals, right?"

Beep.

"Sure, Dan, everybody likes animals."

"And there's nothing illegal about someone calling me at work to tell me that they want to go to the zoo to pet some animals."

"Dan, that's the most ridiculous thing I've ever heard."

Beep.

"No, hear me out," he said. "Say there's a week when you want to bet the Lions. What you do is call me and tell me that you want to go to the zoo and pet the Lions."

Beep.

"Then you tell me how many times you want to pet the Lions."

"Wait just a minute, Dan," I said. "Time-out."

Beep.

"How about the teams that aren't animals, genius? Am I supposed to tell you that I want to go to the zoo to pet the

49ers? If I want to bet the Jets, do I tell you I want to go to the airport to pet the airplanes?"

Beep.

"Very funny, asshole. No, that's not how it works. When I'm at the desk, you can't bet on teams that aren't animals."

Beep.

Like I said, Danny had it all figured out.

Anyway, you know how this story ends. But no matter how many times Dan fucks up, I'll always be there for him. He burned through his first set of teeth, and I'm sure he'll burn through the next set I buy him, but I'm not even mad. If you run into him at one of my shows or book signings—which will only happen in New Jersey, by the way, because Dan doesn't travel far—let me know what's left of that second set of choppers. Everyone deserves a second chance, especially when it comes to teeth.

These days I pay Dan's rent too, which costs me twelve hundred bucks a month. I found this arrangement easier than watching him do the same song and dance for me every thirty days year in and year out. I just put him on my payroll, so now he picks up his rent from my business manager on the first of the month and leaves me alone. I'm happy to do it, because he'd be on the street otherwise. No one else he knows can afford to support him, so I do, because that's what best friends are for.

Every once in a while, I wonder how Dan's life would have turned out if the Giants had covered. Would he have gone to college and graduated? What would he have studied? Would he have ended up addicted to drugs and destroyed his life anyway? Probably, but I believe that being a cop sent him deeper into drugs because he witnessed horrors that no one is equipped to deal with. He covered a pretty rough neighborhood rife with drugs and crime and told me stories that I could barely process. It was the kind of place where, more than once, he and his partner found the remains of an infant that a junkie had killed by putting it in a microwave because it cried too much. He saw that *more than once.* There's no way to prepare yourself for that.

When you're a cop, you become jaded or you go crazy; there's no other way to survive the job. Danny numbed himself out with drugs, alcohol, and strippers. He was always fucking strippers, which is a lot of fun for a night or two, but when it becomes a habit, it starts to erode your soul. I don't blame him at all because I would have done the same thing. There was a strip club called Knockers exactly one block from his precinct, for Christ's sake. I'm not kidding; it was really called Knockers. That is where he would have breakfast most mornings after doing the midnight-to-8:00 a.m. shift. Knockers opened early for the cops and anyone else who wanted to see strippers first thing in the morning, which was very considerate. They even had a special they called something like "Legs and Eggs," or maybe it was "Tits and Grits." It was breakfast and boobs for the boys in blue. The owner of Knockers knew the score, because after a nice hot meal and a lap dance, any cop who went for breakfast at a strip club was going to look the other way when he saw girls giving blow jobs in the parking lot.

6

INJUN GIVER

This one kid I worked with at Port Newark hosted a poker night that was always a dealer's choice game. Four or five of us would go, real guys' guys, and we'd play five-card draw, seven-card stud, real guy games. This was long before every jerk-off in the world started playing Texas Hold'em, trying to be as cool as James Bond in *Casino Royale*. You know how that happened? Ben Affleck played Texas Hold'em once for charity on Bravo's *Celebrity Poker*, and after that, every fag in the country wanted to be just like Ben. It's ridiculous how that game has become some rite of passage. It's now considered a test of your skill at cards, and it really shouldn't be.

Straight poker has always been a better game than Texas Hold'em. Five-card draw, five-card stud, that's what real men play, because those games involve true gambling: raising, not raising, bluffing your opponent. People say that about Texas Hold'em, but they're wrong. People who prefer

Texas Hold'em can't handle the swings that are at the heart of real poker. Sure, the turns in Texas Hold'em are on the flip cards, so you can go from having the biggest fortune to nothing at all, which is enough to make it too dangerous for most people. That kind of swing from all to nothing thrills the true gambler, but it's also not as dangerous to them as it is to the average Hold'em player. A lot of people don't think there's skill involved in riding those waves, but there is because if you're a practiced gambler, you know how to read your opponents, so the swings don't surprise you—you plan for them. If you aren't able to constantly read your opponents while playing the game, you shouldn't be playing any type of poker at all. Stick to Go Fish or War. Did you know that they actually have tables where you can play War in Vegas? I know this because I caught a couple of the guys who worked on Howard's TV show playing it when we were out there. I waited for them to finish up and called them over and said, "Never do that again. What you did isn't immoral, but it is deeply embarrassing. If you can't help yourselves and you need to play War, never tell anyone about it."

I can read people well enough to win card games, but winning that way doesn't thrill me. When I play cards, reading my opponents is never my primary strategy, not because it's not a good one but because it's much less exciting than betting and playing the game. I'd rather try to manipulate the other players with bets or bluffs or other behavior. I'd rather just play and let chance do its thing than sit there on a stakeout all night. Some people are so proud of their ability to read people, however. Usually they'll mention it as some kind of warning, like they're doing you a favor. Usually I tell them, "That's good to know, man. Can you tell what I'm thinking right now? Here's a hint: *Fuck you.*" Or I break out a joke I used to do in my act. For those who don't know, when you play cards, a *tell* is an involuntary gesture that gives players away when they've got a good hand. It can be an extra blink of the eye or the twitch of a cheek. Players who go that route pride themselves on reading tells and having none. So I used to say, "I love playing cards, but my tell always gives me away. When I get a great card, I violently shit my pants."

The movie *Rounders* is the first movie Matt Damon did after *Good Will Hunting*, which is easy to forget, because he did five movies in a row where he played a genius. Anyway, in that movie, John Malkovich plays a Russian gangster who has a tell that Malkovich later admitted was a goof he improvised. His accent in the movie had to be a goof too, because he's such a good actor, but in *Rounders* he sounds like Yakov Smirnoff playing a hit man. In the film, Malkovich's character is unbeatable because he has a tell no one in the underground gambling club can figure out. His character also likes to eat Oreo cookies while he plays. At the end of the movie, which is about two hours long, Matt Damon figures out what everyone else, conceivably for years, has missed. He realizes that the Malkovich character's tell is that he eats an Oreo cookie. Usually a guy scratches his nose or rubs his eye, but no, this Russian thug eats a cookie. And you should see him do it: he takes it apart, he eats the middle, he really takes his time with it. I can't think of a more obvious tell. It's the most ridiculous thing any card player has ever been asked to believe. Norm Macdonald used to do a joke about it, and in one deadpan punch line he proved how bad that movie sucked. "Have you seen *Rounders*? The guy who eats Oreos while he plays eats an Oreo when he gets a good card. Now that's a tough table."

Anyway, this kid I worked with at the port hosted card games at his house in Down Neck, and we weren't high rollers but we all liked gambling, so the pots got pretty big. Back then, Down Neck was protected, and still is, which means that no one fucks with people in Down Neck. That neighborhood is justifiably featured quite a bit in *The Sopranos*, if you know what I'm trying to say. It's located close to what locals call the Pasta Triangle, comprised of Bloomfield, Belleville, and Nutley. Satriale's Pork Store is right around where I hung out, as are a lot of other *Sopranos* locations. That show is understandably hooked into those neighborhoods. They even mentioned the chicken savoy at the Belmont Tavern, which is a dish that celebrities, popes, and politicians have come from far and wide to enjoy since the '60s. It's delicious, by the way: chicken on the bone baked with herbs and cheese and sprinkled with red vinegar.

The last scene in *The Sopranos* took place at Holsten's, which is an ice cream parlor in Bloomfield that I grew up going to because my cousin lived around the corner. I ate hot dogs and ice cream in the booth where Tony is last seen before the screen fades to black for the last time, leaving you unsure of whether he lives or dies. Despite the non-Italian name, Holsten's is a very Italian place, so during that final scene, as I watched Tony and his family sitting there, I thought that if he were going to be whacked, it would be by someone who shouldn't be at Holsten's. I was watching the finale with my cousin, and he agreed with my theory, so we started looking at everyone in the scene, every extra sitting in the background, everyone coming and going, watching for someone who was out of place. About halfway through, four black kids come through the door.

"See anything that doesn't look right?" I asked. "Anything that looks odd?"

We both started laughing because in all the years we went there, there was never a black kid in Holsten's. Not that they weren't allowed in; they just didn't come. It was an unspoken mutual agreement that we were pretty sure hadn't been amended.

So that's Down Neck and the Triangle for you.

Let's get back to this card game. As I mentioned, it was a dealer's choice game, and when it came around to our host's turn to deal, he always called Injun Poker. I want to be clear about this: he meant Injun as in Native American *woo-woo* Indian. The rest of us made fun of him for it, because that is the gayest name for a card game, and it's a pretty ridiculous game. It's also very racist, but that's beside the point.

Here's how you play. Everyone is dealt one card, facedown. Everyone puts that card up against their foreheads, facing out. That is apparently supposed to represent a feather, as if you're a Native American. See, I told you it's stupid. You can't see your own card; you can only see what everyone else in the game has. And then you start betting.

You guess blindly, while trying to figure out where you stack up. You have to look around, take stock of the cards on your opponents' heads, and try to figure out if they know what they have. It's ridiculous. If you find yourself in a game of Injun and see a lot of high cards when you look around, my advice is to bow out immediately. When you bow out, you say, "One, two, three, out," then you bend over and lay your card down on the table so you can't see it until the round is over. People will call you a pussy because if you're out, you don't owe anything. If you stay in and you lose, you owe the pot, which means that you have to match whatever is in the pot when the winner is declared. If there's a grand in the pot when you go up against someone and lose, you pay that out and match that grand to refill the pot. If two guys lose to one guy, each of them owe the pot, so the winner gets his and the pot gets even bigger.

That is how the pots get heavy in what is a pretty juvenile game, because even if none of the players are high rollers, things escalate quickly. Say there's two grand in there and you beat the last two guys. You get the two grand, then they put in two thousand each, making four thousand the starting pot for the next round. There is potential for a lot of money to be thrown around, which is exactly what happened to us, because the host of this card game was a pretty smart hustler working a long con. As much as we made fun of him for it, after a few months we got used to him calling Injun when it was his turn to deal. And once we were used to it, he made his move. One night the game really got hot, and the pot hit an all-time high of $32,000. He stayed in, he won, and he took it all. The rest of us were floored because that was a lot of money to us. If it were me looking around at the downtrodden faces of my friends, I wouldn't have kept it all, but not him.

A couple of the guys took it really hard. They told him

flat out that he had completely busted them and that they would not be able to play cards, go drinking, or do anything but work and stay home for quite a while. It was fucking awkward. But he stood strong; he didn't give a fuck or one dollar back. What could we do? We congratulated him. It was gambling, but as much as we loved it, the card games stopped because after that night we couldn't afford them. It took months for the rest of us to be back in the black and ready for cards again, all of us wanting to win some of our money back from that kid.

The games took place at a big round table in his front room. It was in a nook surrounded by windows, nothing special, and the way that friends do when they gather to play cards, we always sat in the same seats. Whether it's superstition or tradition, that's card player etiquette when you have a standing game with the same people. That reunion night, however, I sat down in our host's seat. I think he was in the bathroom or something, and it had been a while, so I'd forgotten where I used to sit. It didn't matter, anyway, because we hadn't started playing. We always ordered food at the beginning of the night and ate it before we got the cards out. So I was sitting there eating a sub sandwich like a disgusting guttersnipe when I looked up and clear as day, saw my reflection in the window looking back at me, eating a sub sandwich. I could make out every detail as if it were a mirror. From that distance, I could even see the color of my eyes.

Wow, I thought. *Isn't that something, you motherfucker.*

The fucking guy had cheated. He'd scouted out the table, he'd always left the blinds up, and he'd been working us for months. My mind started reeling trying to figure out how many times he'd won compared to the rest of us. Obviously, the last game stuck out. I dropped my sandwich and got the other guys' attention as quietly as I could. Before he came back in the room, I made a few of them sit there, and we all agreed that if we were sitting there playing Injun, and had a card up against our head, we'd be able to see it easily in that window.

How do you think that went over? The guy who took home $32,000 knew his card and what he was betting with the entire time. To tell you the truth, as much as it sucked for me, I thought his victory was funny. Who the hell wins thirty-two grand playing Injun? Two or three of the other guys didn't quite feel the same. They were real Newark Italian kids who didn't take kindly to bullshit. I hadn't known our host for long, but they'd grown up with him and felt completely betrayed and disrespected. They were right, of course: it was a fucked-up, insulting thing to do to your friends for the kind of cash that really affected their lives. I watched as everyone in that room realized just how calculated his play had been. The guys who had known him longest wanted to kill him or at least permanently harm him. The time between me realizing his trick to me telling everyone about it to him coming back in the room happened real fast, so they didn't have time to unanimously decide how severely to injure him. I do remember one kid sitting there, bristling with anger, looking like Psycho from *Stripes*.

"That motherfucker," he said. "I ain't going to jail for killing him because he ain't worth it, but we need to break fingers. I'm talking two, three fingers. Don't you guys worry about it; I'll do it."

He returned from the bathroom and found us staring him down like it was a mob meeting and he was the rat, which he was. We confronted him, and he didn't even try to deny it; he put his head down and started crying. He told us how he was down and out because of gambling debts and how he needed the money. That was not a good argument.

"We would have loaned it to you, dude!" I said. "Why steal from us and make us feel like jerk-offs? You could have slowly paid us back. Instead you robbed your friends."

For months we'd been calling him a loser for calling Injun, but we were the losers, slowly conned, until the moment of truth when he stayed in with a two and took home all our money. We had told everyone we knew the story, about this guy's luck and how we were all broke now. As much as we hated him for it, to us he'd won it fair and square. We liked to gamble, and this was a pretty remarkable gambling story. We were also all friends, so never for a minute did we think that he had fucked us. That night we realized exactly who the guy was and who he always will be.

In the early '90s, Colin Quinn used to do a great bit that relates to this. In the old days, stockbrokers were WASPs, really blue blood types, but in the late '80s, as Colin pointed out, things changed. Movies like *Boiler Room* and *The Wolf of Wall Street* make it pretty clear that suddenly you didn't need skill, brains, tact, or an education. You just needed balls and the ability to lie like a pro. All you had to do was get your clients to buy stocks, because there were no checks and balances. Those illegal boiler rooms became so successful that the best players went legit, and places like Morgan Stanley started hiring guys like the one who used to host the card game.

That's what happened to him. No one killed him, no one broke his fingers, but none of us talked to him after that. He lost his friends, he left the port, and he went on to become one of those guys with a phone and a desk in a back-alley New Jersey boiler room. He had the gambling bug worse than any of us, and if you've got it, it's like herpes: you never get rid of it. He was an excellent liar, so he was great at selling crap stocks and was eventually able to make the jump into the legit world as a broker for Morgan Stanley. But, long story short, he ended up being convicted for securities fraud, losing his license, and doing time. I'm not sure of the extent of his illegal activity, but I'd bet it was excessive, because he was the type who couldn't help cheating the system, even when he had it all. He spent just about all the money he'd made that wasn't seized to hire a good lawyer, so in the end he did less than a year in jail, but he lost his livelihood forever.

None of us who played Injun with him were surprised when we read about it in the local paper. It's weird; I've done some pretty depraved things, but I've always maintained a code of honor when it comes to money, which is the only reason I'm not dead or in jail right now. No matter how fucked up I've been, I've always paid the people that count: the government, drug dealers, bookies, hookers, and loan sharks. My old man always said that whatever you do, you have to pay your bills. He was right, because if you do that, nobody fucks with you. If your dope dealer is a good businessman who shows up when he says he will and fronts you when you need him to, then pay him back quickly. Do that and you'll have no problems. Lucky for me, I became a junkie when I had enough money to cover my debts. I've never been as desperate as the kid who ripped off his friends. The saddest part of the story is that he could have borrowed it from us, or from a shylock, which would have been better than ripping us off, which was inexcusable.

He's still alive today, by the way, and in the AA program, because all the vices add up since they all come from the same place. Whatever form it takes, addiction is nothing if not an endless pit of wanting. If you're an addict, no matter how much you have, you always want more. We had so many vices on display at those poker games it's astonishing. I remember playing Injun, a drink at my side, holding my card to my head with one hand while bending down to do a line of coke through a bill with the other hand. I'm pretty clumsy and usually got coke on my card, so when I returned to an upright position, the guys would give me shit about wasting drugs. There was so much blow going around that you'd have to specify that you weren't bowing out of the round, you were just doing a line. Of course, some people would bluff; they'd do a line and drop their card or turn it over "by mistake" while they were doing it and "accidentally" see it. Yeah, all kinds of bullshit, but even with that, the party-giver still scammed us. There were so many ways to fuck with each other and work the game all in good fun, but that kid was brutal. He was always going to be exactly who he was, the guy swindling his buddies by hosting a crooked game of Injun.

7

MY TWO UNCLES

My uncle Frank and my uncle Pat are two of the most hilarious and important figures in my life. My father died when I was nineteen, so they have been father figures to me ever since. They taught me some very important lessons, mainly not to give a fuck about what anyone thinks and to be myself. They taught me to risk it all for what I believe in. They also thought I was a complete idiot.

My uncle Frank has been a well-respected member of the carpenters' union for years. He's one of the pit bosses, telling all the members in his division who to vote for in each election and generally everything else they should be doing with their lives. He's quite the character; I've watched him yell at people but not remember what he's supposed to be telling them to do. I wasn't in his union, but he didn't care; he'd tell me who to vote for to support his cause, and it usually went something like this.

"Listen, you jerk-off, I've got the fuckin' list; here's what you're gonna do for me today."

"All right, Uncle Frank, what am I doing?"

"Fuggin' write this down. Vote all this shit is what you're gonna do; you vote Palucci on number 6. Palucci and Reggerio. Vote Reggerio, vote Macallaly, Reggerio."

"Who?"

"What do you mean, who? Listen to me. Wait, that's wrong. What the fuck does this paper say? Oh yeah, vote Tonelli. That's with a *T*. Oh, fuck, no it's Canelli! Canelli with a *C*, like *cunt*. Vote Canelli. Vote Frantantoni. Danny Anamato. Vote him too."

"Got it, Uncle Frank. I should vote for Steve Anamato."

"No! What's wrong with you? That's his brudda! Steve Anamato, he's dead. Don't vote him; don't get us in trouble now. Don't let them see you vote for a dead guy, you fuck. You get caught voting for a dead guy, you'll fuck up the whole thing."

"Okay, Uncle Frank, I got it. No dead guys. It's Danny Anamato. His brother was a greater statesman, though, don't you think?"

"You jerk-off, you don't think, you do what I tell you to!"

I used to make extra money doing odd jobs for my uncle, which was great but also a source of constant aggravation for the both of us. I never seemed to get it right, so he was never happy with me. That never bothered me, because when Uncle Frank was giving me shit, he said some of the funniest things I've ever heard in my life. In terms of doing better, this was precisely the wrong type of incentive for me, because it was hard to want to please him when disappointing him was so fucking funny.

Take, for example, the time he had me Sheetrock the bathroom of an associate's goomah. For those who don't know, that's Italian American slang for a mistress.

"Artie, you are so stupid, yet you live. I told you to fucking Sheetrock my friend's goomah's bathroom. It looks like shit! I gotta fucking hear it from him and from her now. Terry Fackineri's bathroom. Did you do Terry Fackineri's bathroom?"

"I did, Uncle Frank; I did it like you told me."

"Show some fucking respect! The Sheetrock is uneven! What the fuck is wrong with you? Whaddya got bad eyes?"

Along with "Artie, you don't fish; you're too fat to fish," "Artie, you're so stupid, yet you live," is the funniest thing anyone has ever said to me. My mother said the first, my uncle said the second. That's my family!

Here's another conversation Uncle Frank and I had all the time. It involved a guy that Uncle Frank had some kind of feud with. His opponent, the source of his aggravation, would change all the time, but the conversation remained the same. I never knew what the beef was about; all I knew was that Uncle Frank wanted to know what the guy did when I mentioned Uncle Frank's name. This was very, very important to him.

"Did you go to that job?"

"Yeah."

"Did you see that guy?"

"Yeah, I saw him."

"What'd he say?"

I'd tell him what the guy said.

"What'd you say?"

I'd tell him what I said.

"What'd he do?"

I'd tell him what he did.

"What'd you do?"

I'd tell him what I did.

"What'd he say when you did that?"

I'd tell him what he said when I did that.

"Fuck him. He's a jerk-off."

This started when I was about seventeen and would have continued until today if I'd stayed working at the port. Uncle Frank would tell me to go find the guy, whatever guy it was at the time, and he'd tell me exactly what to go and say to the guy. Sometimes it would be just mentioning his name, intended, I assume, to strike fear in the guy. So I'd go and shout Uncle Frank's name from a distance, and things would get awkward as all these carpenters and longshoremen turned around to look at me, wondering what my fucking problem was. I'd see Uncle Frank a few weeks later, and, as usual, we'd have the same conversation again.

"You see that guy?"

"What'd he say?"

"Then what'd you say?"

"Then what'd he do?"

"Then what'd you do?"

"Then what'd he say when you did that?"

"He's a jerk-off."

Six months later, I'd see him. "C'mere, asshole. How you been? You see that guy?"

Every time, it was identical. I'd say, "Uncle Frank, you realize you're asking about the same guy you asked about last time I saw you."

"Oh, Jesus, I'm thinking of your brudda."

I'm not joking, this is my job.

I'm Artie Lange and you're not!

AT LEFT: I promised famous Chicagoan Dan Falato that if his Cubs won the World Series, he could shove two fingers in my ass. Needless to say, I keep my promises! In 107 years, he can do it again.

BELOW: Here is some Artie Lange trivia: One of these guys is a former NBA player.

ABOVE: Unfortunately, ticket sales aren't always great!

AT LEFT: Me playing at the great Wilbur Theater in Boston. The first chick I ever fucked looked like David Ortiz—and he spoke better English.

ABOVE: Me standing in my favorite state, overlooking my favorite city.

AT LEFT: The only thing better than having Anthony Bozza as your coauthor is having him as a friend. You're looking at a hell of a successful team.

AT RIGHT: After hours and hours of begging me on the set of *Crashing*, I finally let Gina Gershon take a picture with me. If she would stop being so clingy, she could become Mrs. Gina Lange.

BELOW: Dan Falato took this picture after I played Foxwoods Casino. This is what happens when you use a craps system invented by Norm Macdonald.

DANIEL FALATO

DANIEL FALATO

TOP: Me at *The Tonight Show* with the person I want to be when I grow up, my beautiful sister Stacey

BOTTOM LEFT: This is the reason I can't judge Joel Osteen, and to the victims of Hurricane Sandy, you should have brought your own ferry!

BOTTOM RIGHT: Here I receive the word from Pete Holmes on the set of *Crashing* that his wedding will not be open bar.

BRUCE CAPRIO

DANIEL FALATO

ABOVE LEFT: A night out for my mother's birthday. Here she turned seventy and I looked seventy-one.

ABOVE RIGHT: Here I am preparing to do Don Lemon's show on CNN. This is also the night I found out Don Lemon was black.

BELOW: Guineas in Paris: Me, Anthony Bozza, and Dan Falato.

ANTHONY BOZZA

DANIEL FALATO

DANIEL FALATO

TOP: Here I am with some of the funniest people alive and Dave Juskow. Dave Attell, Russ Meneve, and Dave Juskow. I love you all.

INSET: This has nothing to do with the book, but here I am with the hilarious Fred Willard.

BOTTOM: I didn't realize when I met Dan Falato just a few years ago that he would become one of the best friends I've ever had. BTW, Rutgers doesn't have enough black guys.

"Uncle Frank, I don't have a brother."

"Shut up. The grill is hot; go help your mother with the sausages."

Even when I started to make up conversations that I'd had with "the guy" to entertain myself, the conversation remained the same. No matter how far I took it, no matter how absurd or insulting of a remark or action I came up with that "the guy" had said or done, Uncle Frank always ended up saying the same thing: "He's a jerk-off."

My uncle Pat is also one in a million. One year we got him tickets to see *Cats* on Broadway, which was the biggest show running at the time. After he had seen it, I asked him if he liked it.

"The fucking play is all about cats," he said.

"Well, yeah, Uncle Pat, it's called *Cats*."

"No, no, no. You don't get it. They're dressed like cats. The show is fifty faggots dressed like cats."

"But that's why they call it *Cats*. What did you think it was going to be about?"

"I thought it was a symbolic thing. Don't be a jerk-off. There were no dogs in *Dog Day Afternoon*!"

I don't think I've ever laughed harder. I told that story to Norm Macdonald, and the same day, he turned around and told it on *Letterman*, acting like it was his joke. It was blatant plagiarism, but I can't blame him; Uncle Pat is hilarious.

Uncle Frank used to claim that he drove the car that carried the guy who carried out the hit on Connie Francis's brother. I have no idea if that was a joke, but I'd always tell him not to tell me anything more about that. Also, here's how he gives directions.

"Uncle Frank, how do I get there?"

"It's down the shore. I don't know how you get there. You are so stupid. Did you go take the retard test? Your mother's very bright. Your sister's very bright. I don't know what's wrong with you. Okay, you wanna know where it is? Go down the parkway, make a left, you'll be there. There's a shine, works at the Exxon station, he knows the whole fucking area."

Shine, by the way, is a very old-school racist term for an African American. It's Uncle Frank's preferred racial slur.

The other uncle that I learned about comedy from wasn't a blood uncle at all; his name was Sonny and he was what we call a "neighborhood uncle." He was even funnier than Uncle Frank and Uncle Pat and never realized it. He was so Italian that I'd find him at home with a tomato in one hand and a mozzarella in the other, taking bites from each of them like they were apples. I told a story about him on *Letterman*, and it was the hardest I've ever made Dave laugh. And to think that I almost didn't tell it!

It was my fifth appearance on the show, and the same segment producer, who was a really nice kid, handled me every time I went in. At that point I was still very intimidated, because I'd been such a huge fan of Letterman for so long. How could I not be? He's the funniest, wittiest guy to do late night in my lifetime. So I told the segment producer the story I'm about to tell you, and he told me not to do it.

"It's a little offensive," he said. "Dave likes to keep it clean. We're not in the old 12:30 time slot anymore."

"Really? I think he'd like it because it's something my

uncle really said, and he likes when people talk about their families, right?"

"I think you should skip it."

I told him I would, but when I went on, I did so well that my confidence was at an all-time high. Sitting in that chair, with Dave behind his desk, I said fuck it and decided to go for it. I waited until we were toward the end of my time slot and found some way to crowbar my uncle into whatever we were talking about. I even stopped Dave from going to commercial, which was a huge risk. I saw his eyes roll a little bit, as if to say, "This had better be good." If the story sucked, my whole appearance would have been a failure and my chance of returning would have been uncertain, because Dave did not suffer fools.

So I told Dave about my uncle who is so Italian that he eats tomatoes and mozzarella like they're apples, and I told him how every once in a while, he really surprises me. I told him how one day I went to his house to visit when he was about eighty–three years old (he has since passed away) and when I came in the room he shushed me because he was glued to the TV.

"Uncle Sonny, what are you watching?" I asked.

"*Buffy the Vampire Slayer,*" he said.

"Oh yeah? You like *Buffy the Vampire Slayer*?"

"Yeah, it's a great show."

"Oh yeah? Uncle Sonny, what's it about?"

"A Jew broad who fights Draculas."

Letterman completely lost it. He laughed so hard he rolled the fucking chair back. That punch line got such a huge laugh into a solid, long applause break that all he could do was signal to send the show to commercial; he was laughing too hard to say, "We'll be right back." Once we were off air, he leaned over to me, still chuckling, and said, "That's the funniest fucking thing I've ever heard."

The segment producer, who was a little effeminate, came up to me afterward and admitted that it was a great story. That kid was what my uncle Frank would call "flimsy," which was his term for "light in the loafers," if you know what I mean. "That guy there is fucking flimsy, man."

He actually once called Flip Wilson "a flimsy shine." He was watching Flip Wilson, who by anyone's standards was a man's man, in drag, playing his mother in a comedy bit, and he called him a "flimsy shine." He didn't recognize Flip, and I'll never forget it. Could there be a more offensive phrase? Think about our world today. With just two words, my uncle successfully marginalized and offended millions of people.

"Flimsy shine": such a simple phrase, so full of prejudice and judgment. It's also a great name for a TV show. "Aziz Ansari is *Flimsy Shine*. Wednesdays at nine." Aziz should do it; it would be the funniest thing he ever does. But he never would, because he'd lose his audience. They're much too sensitive for something that satirical and sarcastic. He'd go from playing Madison Square Garden to my career.

But it would be classic must-see TV. "Later, on an all-new *Flimsy Shine*—can Flimsy deal with *racism*?" "Next week, Flimsy deals with his worst nightmare, racism, and its ugly cousin, *homophobia*." "Stay tuned! After touring a zoo, Flimsy gets trapped on a bus, stuck in a deadly enclosure, alone, with a dead bus driver and one other passenger. That passenger is Flimsy's worst nightmare: he's not only *racist*, he's *homophobic*. Don't miss a special episode of *Flimsy Shine* starring Aziz Ansari, with special guest Artie Lange as Racist Homophobe Harry. And later, an all-new *Jew Broad Who Fights Draculas*."

8

KEEF FOR PRESIDENT

I've been playing the Borgata in Atlantic City twice a year
since 2006, so the big room there is like a second home
to me. It holds 3,500 people, and I always sell it out, sometimes two shows in one night, so the promoters and hotel
staff treat me very well. In 2007, I noticed that the Rolling
Stones were playing, and the Borgata was a sponsor, so I
called my connection down there and made arrangements
to bring a girl I was seeing and a couple of friends. They
hooked me up with a suite at the hotel, VIP tickets; full
rock star treatment.

The Stones were playing the sold-out Atlantic City
Convention Center, which holds fifteen thousand people,
and I couldn't wait, because, along with Springsteen, the
Stones are my favorite rock-and-roll band. We got down
to the hotel, checked in, and when it was showtime, a concierge brought us through a back entrance, directly to the
VIP seats, which were in the front rows, less than ten feet

from the stage. I was even more excited, because I knew we were on Keith Richards's side. Directly in front of us, I noticed one of the kids from *That '70s Show* who isn't Ashton Kutcher sitting with one of the Olsen twins—I believe the one with two names—but who can really tell? They were smoking a joint, which they shared with us, and it was some of the strongest weed I've ever smoked in my life. It hit me immediately, so as I sat there trying to act casual, inside I was freaking out. With my mind reeling, I kept looking at this teeny-tiny waif of a girl with a giant handbag, puffing away at this thing like it was a Marlboro Light while I, the notorious drug addict, had a silent panic attack after one hit.

I lit a cigarette to try to calm down and thought about how much I love the Stones, especially Keith Richards. He has seen it all, done it all, and he keeps going, pushing the envelope well into his seventies. All my favorite artists, from John Belushi to Richard Pryor, attacked their art the way they lived their lives: they never played it safe, and they took no quarter. And Keith Richards is . . .

"Excuse me, sir. You can't smoke here."

. . . the epitome of . . .

"Sir! You deaf? You can't smoke here."

I turned around to find a security guard, who was Puerto Rican and in his midthirties, staring at me.

"Listen, Artie, I'm sorry about this, but you can't smoke in here," he said.

"C'mon, man, are you serious?" The smoke from Olsen's joint was still hanging over her like Los Angeles smog, but he was giving me shit?

"I know these are VIP seats, but everyone is looking at

you. This is my section, and it's my ass if somebody sees you smoking and word gets back to my supervisor."

"I hear ya, but listen, I really need a cigarette," I said, hoping that a sympathy play would win him over. It didn't, because they never do.

"No one can smoke in here anymore, man. The fucking president can't smoke if he comes here to watch a show."

Through the strong stench of weed, I caught a distinct whiff of bullshit. "You mean to tell me that if the president of the United States was here, he wouldn't be able to smoke?"

"That's right. Those are the rules."

"You mean to tell me that Keith Richards isn't going to be allowed to have a cigarette while he's onstage playing tonight?"

"Nope. Not even him."

The guy proceeded to explain, in a very long-winded fashion, how everyone in the Rolling Stones camp was told that under no circumstances were they to smoke onstage. This was ridiculous, because anyone who has ever seen the Stones knows that both Keith and Ronnie Wood smoke while they're onstage. A cigarette is part of Keith's gear; it's synonymous with him the way big sunglasses are synonymous with Bono. It would shock fans if he didn't light up during a show.

"So let me get this straight," I said. "Neither Keith Richards or Ronnie Wood are going to have a cigarette the entire time they're onstage?"

"No."

"Neither of them?"

"No."

"Are you a gambling man?" I asked.

"Definitely; I also work for the casino, you know."

"Well, I bet you $1,000 that Keith Richards has a cigarette while he's playing tonight."

"You're on!" he said. "I don't give a shit if you're a VIP, Artie; I'll take your money!"

"You got it on you? Because I've got it on me."

"No, but I can get it back at the hotel."

"All right, then, man, you're on!"

As if the night couldn't get better, now I had some action going. Action gives meaning to a degenerate gambler's life. It brings excitement to things that are otherwise dull and boring, and it makes exciting things even more of a thrill. In this case, it added excitement to something that was already exciting—that's a win-win! I was kidding with the security guard at first, but his smug confidence and obvious lack of knowledge when it came to the Rolling Stones pissed me off. It became personal, and I could tell that I'd had the same effect on him. Deep down, he knew the rules were bullshit, but it was his job to uphold them, so it became personal for him too. And once we had action going, everything changed, because that's what action does. It became me versus him, so if he didn't like me before, he really didn't like me once we had money on the line.

"Artie, just let it go," my date said. "This is awkward now."

"Why? We have a bet going. Don't you want to see what happens? I do!"

"Look at him; he looks really pissed off, Artie," she said. "Why does everything you do have to be so crazy? Nothing can ever be relaxing."

She was right; it was awkward, but that's just the way I'm wired, and she hadn't quite figured that out yet. We were past the point of having a reasonable conversation about it, so now I just wanted to win the bet and teach the guy a lesson. It was the cherry on the sundae for me that night. If my life were a movie, I'd have enjoyed a million happy endings by now, but it's not. My life continues, against the odds, so I have to find ways to keep it exciting; otherwise, I'll die of boredom, wondering what's going to happen next. What should I do, sit around eating egg-white omelets and gluten-free muffins for the rest of my life? Fuck that; I need action, because there isn't anything in the world that can't be made more interesting with the addition of a little action.

The lights went down, the crowd roared, and the opening riff of "Satisfaction" reverberated through the hall. As the lights came up, a spotlight shone on Keith, who was standing directly in front of me. There he stood, in a circle of light, hunched over, laying down that classic guitar line with a lit Marlboro Red 100 in his mouth as a thick blue cloud of smoke curled around his head.

I looked over at the guard and smiled. The guy looked like he wanted to kill me.

"I'll give you the fucking money at the hotel!" he yelled.

He was so mad that he moved to another part of the section so he didn't have to see me. I was positive that I'd never see him again, and that was fine. I'd won the bet and proven a point—two things that mattered more to me than the $1,000. I'd also earned the right to smoke, which I did whenever I wanted for the rest of the concert.

After the show, we went back to the Borgata, and after

hanging out in the suite for a bit, my girl and I went down-
stairs to play craps. Norm Macdonald had taught me his system for playing craps, and that night I wanted to give it a
shot. Norm always plays the Don't Pass line, which means
you're betting against the roller, so you win when they roll
a seven or crap out. A lot of people consider that taboo or
in bad taste, and a lot of gamblers call it "playing the dark
side," because you win when the other players lose. It's very
Norm: he'd be winning, doubling his bets and celebrating
as the rollers continued to lose. You need a big bankroll to
play this system, because you can lose a lot of money in a
hurry, but as Norm always says, when it comes to gambling, "You've gotta lose money to make money." Norm
always counted on losing but at some point in the night
going on a big run that would put him ahead.

We'd been down there about four hours when the security
guard found me at the tables. I didn't recognize him in his
street clothes, and to be honest, I'd forgotten all about him.

"Here's your money, asshole," he said, and he grinned.

"C'mon, man, don't worry about it," I said. "I don't want
to take your money."

I really didn't. He could not be making that much as a
security guard; he was just a regular, hardworking guy.

"Take it," he said. "I'm not a welsher."

I respected that. Growing up in Jersey, you were only as
good as your word, especially when it came to betting. It
didn't matter if you were drunk or sober; betting on a big
game or how many wings you could eat in a minute, when
you lost, you paid up, no matter what. I didn't want to dis-
respect him, so I took his money. By that point, I was
going to call it a night, plus my girl wanted to go up to the

room, but when this guy came along with a thousand bucks, I insisted on staying.

"It's free money! I've got to try to win something with this. It's a good omen!"

I told the guard to stay and play craps with me, which he did. I was using Norm's system but wasn't having much luck with it. I wasn't even winning enough to double my bets and start a run, so I kept betting more and more, hoping to fill out my bankroll. I had the guard roll for me and put $5,000 on the Don't Pass. His first roll, the dice came up seven. Fuck me. I put another $5,000 down and had him roll again. He rolled another seven. That sucked, but no problem, I put another $5,000 down, because what were the odds that this goon would roll sevens three times in a row? Slim to none.

He rolled the dice . . . another seven.

I couldn't fucking believe it. Four minutes, three straight sevens, $15,000 gone. It was one of those nights, but since I'm a degenerate gambler, I couldn't let it go. At one point I ran out of cash and had to get an advance on my Amex Platinum card. They did that right at the table for me: the pit boss came over with the paperwork, I signed it, and they brought me the money. It's like getting a bank loan but cooler, because a broad with her tits hanging out brought me free drinks the whole time. Back when I was on *Stern* and playing casinos in Vegas and Atlantic City many times a year, they used to ask me if I wanted to be paid in cash or in credit for the tables—that's how bad I used to be. This night was like a flashback to those days, because I was busted but I wasn't ready to quit. And I didn't quit until I was $26,400 in the hole.

The security guard stayed and watched the whole thing, because he might have lost $1,000 but he won his bosses $26,400.

"You really should get a cut of that," I told him when I finally tore myself away.

For all my trouble, the casino comped me a steak dinner at the all-night restaurant. I wasn't even hungry, but there was no way in hell that I wasn't going to eat that fucking steak. My girl thought the whole thing was pathetic.

"How can you say that?" I asked. "Go to bed if you want, but don't you want to know what a $26,400 steak tastes like?"

9

DIGGING A HOLE

I've appeared on *Late Night with David Letterman* twelve times. I've gone on and absolutely killed, and the first time I did so was one of greatest feelings I've ever known. But I kept going back, so soon enough I knew exactly what type of story to tell and which comments would play best off Dave. Killing on *Letterman* became second nature to me, until eventually I had this conversation with myself, in the green room, about an hour before an appearance.

"*Letterman* again—man, it doesn't get any better than this. But what's different this time? Well, the last time I was here, I did not have a big bag of coke in my pocket. Hey . . . maybe I should do some now, right here in the green room. I can't be the first person to do that. Actually, why *haven't* I done that by now? Jesus Christ, what else do I have to offer them that isn't just Artie again? Know what? I *need* to do some cocaine before this appearance. Dave's audience knows what they're in for with me. I've got to be old news to them by now! If I show them a different Artie, that's new, and they haven't seen Cocaine Artie live on *Dave* yet. Let's think about this: if I do some of the coke, I'll look agitated and high on drugs. That will get ratings, maybe a *Page Six* item. That I can do. But let's think bigger. What if I do the entire bag? I'll look insane, and that would really be something. I could fuck up badly or I could kill. If I do the entire eight ball in the next ten minutes, I'll be so high that who knows what will happen. I might even insult Dave and not even realize it. If I do it all, I might bomb and completely ruin my career."

Obviously, I went for it. It wasn't my best show, and I wasn't asked back for a while, but fuck my minutes in the chair sure were exciting! This behavior doesn't stop when I'm off drugs, by the way. A layman might think it would, but anyone who knows addiction understands that the drive doesn't go away; it just changes forms as you eliminate the need. After I got sober, I did *Letterman* again, and instead of doing cocaine, I ate Twinkies, because there is nothing like a cheap sugar high when you've got type 2 diabetes. You take down a handful of Twinkies and all the corn syrup and chemicals will get you just as light-headed and dopey, and if you take it too far and you're as fat as I am, you'll pass out. When I'm sober, if I don't have an insulin shot with me, I can get momentarily high at any craft service table. That is what you do when you go to any length to make things spontaneous and unpredictable, because that is all that you look forward to in life.

My definition of gambling is making a choice to defy the comfort zone at all costs, and what I've realized is that my favorite bets involve betting with things I can't replace, like my health, my profession, and my relationships. That's the real deal. If you're like me, those are the bets that make you feel most alive. In that arena, innocent junk food consumed might blow your house of cards down or conversely reaffirm your confidence for months to come. Being unsafe like that serves to handicap me so that I can see whether or not I'm still talented enough to haul myself out of the holes I dig for myself. If I can't come from behind and win, I've lost my edge.

I'm not alone in playing this twisted game. Any comic worth seeing more than once tests themselves, but only the best tempt fate like this. How do you think we get so good at fucking with you people? We start by hating ourselves first and foremost. They say you can't really love someone until you learn to love yourself. Well, let me tell you, the same goes for hate.

I can tell you exactly when I learned to feed that self-loathing into my act. I was still terrible at stand-up comedy, but I wasn't going to quit, because my mother had granted me that second chance. Once I left the port and started driving a cab so that I could get into the city, I started getting up wherever they'd have me. One of the many places, and a personal favorite, was CBGB's Gallery. That was the art and performance space next door to the legendary concert venue, and in keeping with the spirit of CB's, anything with attitude was welcome. So I managed to get myself some time—I don't even remember how—but all that I needed to get me in gear was the knowledge that I was going to do a few minutes of comedy in a room somehow related to the Ramones and all the great punk bands that had inspired me so much. They'd all played next door, so for me, two minutes in the basement adjacent to that was a dream come true.

The vibe in the Gallery was still punk rock, and I loved that. Every comic who got up had two minutes to sink or swim, and the crowd really let you know how you were doing. Whatever I was spewing worked well enough that they gave me time, regularly, every Tuesday night. That was my first paying gig in comedy, and I still think it's cool that CBGB's was the first venue in the city that actually paid me to show up. There were other perks to the gig as well, like the pharmaceutical-grade coke the sound guy got from Dee Dee Ramone one night. Maybe he was lying, but holy shit, if he wasn't, I have no idea how Dee Dee or any of them lived day to day. I snorted a few lines and walked off into the night, high as a kite. I had a ton of energy, so I kept walking and walking, all the way to the Port Authority, some sixty blocks to the northwest. It felt like I got there in five minutes.

Those early days, wandering around with everything to lose, trying to make a go of my dream, made me who I am. I experienced liberation when it worked, dread when it didn't, but it was exactly where I wanted to be. During this period of time, I learned who I am, because it's when I learned that I'm funny.

IT TOOK ME YEARS to achieve the command of stand-up that I have now. Working up a new hour of material is a process that starts months before it gets to an audience. I test bits here and there and refine them until it all hangs together. I go over everything until I think it's great, so once I'm on tour, doing some version of the same hour every night, it's yesterday's news to me. That doesn't mean I don't enjoy it; it just means that I'm used to it, which leaves room for boredom. And when that happens, I dig a hole. I'm not special; that is what all good comics do to keep themselves at the top of their game. When you're working on new material and you're not sure if it's good, get a shovel and start digging—you'll find out soon enough.

Digging myself into a hole onstage is the creative jolt I have to have. One of my favorite exercises is showing up unannounced at the Comedy Cellar in New York, and if he's around, sometimes Dave Attell will come with me. We will arrive at 1:00 or 2:00 a.m. on a weekend when all the tourists and college kids are drunk, and we make fun of each other, ourselves, and everyone in the audience until every last person gets up and leaves.

It's a great time! I've cleared rooms, but Dave Attell is a master who can clear a room as easily as he can fill it. His true brilliance is doing both in the same set, which is the ultimate comedy high, in my opinion. Deciding to do that is like taking action on your own set, and you know how I feel about taking action.

My friend Nick Di Paolo, who is angry and hates himself more than anyone I know, enjoys going all-in as well. He and I did a tour together a few years ago, and the second we got bored of killing night after night, we started playing a little game. Once you know which jokes in your set work every time, you consider those your safe material. They don't need pacing, they don't need a long setup; pull them out at any time and you'll get your laughs. The unsafe stuff is what you want to focus on because it's still raw and you don't know how it's going to do. That's the problem with younger comedians nowadays; they're all cowards who are afraid to fail. They work out a safe set of material that does not offend, and they stick to it like a script. They've missed the point, because the only way you get better is by failing. They don't understand that because they're spineless PC zombies who were raised on selfies. It doesn't make any sense to me, because young people are so easy to offend, but at the same time, they can't be shocked. Thanks to the internet, they've seen everything and are incredibly blasé about out-there shit, but if you make them deal with something in real life, they get offended. If you force them to think about things, and put those things in their faces, they get traumatized and horrified because they can't handle it.

On most college campuses, all I have to say is "Bruce Jenner has a pussy," and the crowd will go nuts, and not in a good way. To them, Bruce Jenner is the face of transgender identity politics. To me, he's the guy who won the decathlon at the 1976 Olympics. Big difference! You're telling me that the guy with the gold medal that used to be on my Wheaties box when I was a kid has a pussy? I need a couple of seconds to adjust to that information. A sixty-year-old guy gets a pussy and the next day causes a pileup on the highway. I don't think that was a coincidence. Talk about distracted driving; I think he was playing with his new pussy. What male cop wouldn't understand that?

"You killed nine people, Bruce."

"I just got a pussy."

"No shit? You're free to go."

When I do that one, the kids are shocked and the women are appalled. But it's gotten to the point where I've begun to enjoy pissing people off more than I enjoy making them laugh, which is another way of gambling with my career. The stranger and grosser I go with a bit, the more fun I have, because everyone is too fucking sensitive. This generation's Clint Eastwood is Neil Patrick Harris, a gay guy who plays a womanizer on TV. Need I say more? A lot of my comedy isn't about telling jokes; it's about giving people a jolt, which is a lot riskier. And that's why I love it.

Testing new material is like juggling with chain saws for the first time. You could die, or you could do the impossible and pull off a trick they'll never forget. I don't believe in focus groups or dress rehearsals; I believe in delivering the product to the consumers directly to see if they like it. New stuff might bomb, but if you don't have the balls to bomb, you shouldn't be on a stage—you should be in the audience. These young comics today have a seven-minute set that they've worked on for months or years even. They know it kills, and it's exactly what they'll use if they ever get a spot on a talk show. That set will be clean, it will show the world who they are, and in their minds, it might get them a *Seinfeld* sitcom. To them I say, "Whatever, losers. Unfriend me on Facebook."

Those comedians would never dream of digging a hole the way I do. Keep in mind that I consider this fun. I'll get onstage and in the first few minutes say something intended to completely lose me the audience. It is so intentionally offensive on such an unexpected level that, instantly, I'm standing up there alone at the bottom of a fifty-foot pit. That's comforting to me because from there I know my job: to spend the rest of the set climbing out. I try to find a way to win them back, and if it works by the end, I still kill. It's a wild ride, but it doesn't always end well, because sometimes the hole is too deep and my new material isn't strong enough to win the day.

Anyway, I do this by saying the worst thing I can think of as soon as I take the stage. My go-to is always the N-word, but as bad as saying that is, it isn't enough of a shock. So I go further: I say the N-word in a way that it isn't part of a joke; I make it part of me telling a story as if it just so happened to be the word I chose. I say it in a way that is so blatantly racist that it makes everyone instantly uncomfortable. Here's an example.

"I'm sorry I'm late tonight, guys, but on the way here a nigger cut me off."

Another scheme of mine is to tell a truly offensive joke and keep making mistakes telling it, so I end up repeating racial epithets until it gets awkward. That one goes something like this.

"So my uncle told me this joke the other day. Two spics and a nigger walk into a bar . . . wait a minute. I'm sorry, it's *three* spics and *one* nigger . . . okay, wait, that's not it. It's three niggers and a Jew. No, wait, is it *four* niggers? No, no, no, it's four spics and a filthy kike, that's what it is. No, wait, it's one filthy kike, three guineas, and a nigger that walk in to a bar. Wait, four niggers and a . . . yeah, know what? I'll get back to that one."

A few years ago when I toured with Dave Attell and Nick Di Paolo, some nights the three of us would all dig holes to see who climbed out best. I'd do the joke I just told and try not to laugh listening to those two offstage guffawing while a room of uptight people somewhere in Indiana looked at me like I was up there raping someone's grandmother. The gag is that I always eventually abandon the joke, but how long I keep it going depends on how deep a hole I'm after. Some nights I've gone on for quite a while, well past the point of the last uneasy laughs. On those nights when I say, "Never mind, I'll get back to that one," the crowd looks even more horrified. They've just sat through three minutes of racist non sequiturs and got no payoff.

Other nights I'd set the whole thing up as a tribute to my uncle, who never shies away from a racist joke, by the way.

"Hey, guys, it's my uncle's birthday today, so allow me to tell this corny, old-fashioned joke of his. He has told our family this joke around the table every Christmas for as long as I can remember." And then I'd break ground with my shovel and let the indignities fly.

Sometimes, I feel the need to take it even further than that.

"Hey, so my mother told me this joke today, and my mother, she is such a card, she loves this joke. Four niggers are fucking a monkey. No, wait, four monkeys are fucking a nigger. Wait, I'm sorry, this is my mother's joke, so the monkeys are the niggers in this one. Three kikes are fucking four niggers and a monkey—which if you think about it, is really five niggers, right? I think that's how she tells it. No, wait, maybe it's three guineas? You know I am a guinea, so I'm allowed to say that. Anyway, three niggers, a wop, and four kikes are . . . you know what? I'll get back to it; I can't remember how it goes."

No matter how far that gets me from any kind of connection with the audience, it's not enough. I wait until the room is nice and awkwardly silent, then I say something innocuous.

"Anybody here have a CD player? Because mine's on the fritz. I think I need a new one."

"Anyone here ever been to an airport? I mean, *come on*, right?"

Following up racism with the cleanest, most unoriginal comedy bit I can think of always seals the deal. How could it not? What audience wouldn't be wondering where else they could be that night after several minutes of racist slurs followed by "How about those airlines—they're crazy!"

On that tour with Attell and Di Paolo, I was famously the one who dug the deepest hole every night, and my batting average for getting out of it was pretty good. That tour was creative and inspiring, because the three of us tried out new material and approached each audience differently. We had to be at the top of our game or else we'd fail, because we'd started by alienating the crowd.

This used to be a more widespread practice in the stand-up comedy world, but nowadays—thanks to cell phones—people pussy out since everything gets recorded. Put it this way: if Michael Richards wasn't captured by audience members' cell phone cameras, his career would have gone on, because he would have been able to dispute it. Sure, the people that were there that night would stand by what they saw, but without footage there would be doubt. He would have been able to say that he didn't do it or say that they were taking his comments out of context. He could say the whole thing was a bit and that his accusers didn't get it, or that they were just crazy and exaggerating. Hell, without video, he could even say, "Sure, I said *nigger*, but I didn't say it eight times. Who does that?" Even if he admitted it in that way, I think people would have bought it. When you're a celebrity, especially one who played such a beloved character, people want to believe you, but unfortunately you can't refute footage from multiple sources at the scene. When people see something on tape, you're done; they decide for themselves no matter what you say.

Which reminds me of another joke I've used to dig myself into a hole at the start of a set. This one isn't a sure thing, because it paints such a funny picture that it always gets a handful of uncomfortable laughs. It's an awkward one, but it's a good joke on its own. I love this joke, so I do it as a regular bit in my act on nights and in clubs where I feel comfortable, because it's not for everyone or every audience. It's the kind of joke that kills in Boston around midnight—which, if you haven't been there, is a lot like being at a Ku Klux Klan meeting.

Here it is. "How great would it have been if *nigger* was Kramer's catchphrase? Think about it. If every time he did one of those crazy entrances, his catchphrase was *nigger*. 'Oh, I hope Kramer doesn't show up.' *Ahhh-ha!* Nigger!' Jerry and George would be in Jerry's apartment talking and be interrupted by Kramer sliding through the door yelling, 'Nigger'? That would have been great! 'Has anybody seen Kramer?' 'Nuh-nuh-nuh-nigger! Here I am, Jerry!'" It's too bad. If Kramer's catchphrase had been *nigger*, Michael Richards would still have a career.

Digging a hole is a risk, but I see it as necessity. It's what I have to do when stand-up gets boring, because the minute you're complacent doing stand-up comedy is the minute you're through. You have to remain prolific, and you can never rest on your laurels or rely solely on your tried-and-true stuff. You have to be able to read the crowd and adjust accordingly. No matter who they are, you have to find a way to grab their attention and take them with you wherever you want to go. A great act takes timing, good material, and the ability to read the crowd. To continue to be good, you have to stay sharp and be resourceful. George Carlin wrote forty fucking hours of stand-up, which is insane. I have shot three one-hour specials, which I'm proud of since a lot of people stop after they've done just one. I don't plan on slowing down. In fact, I'm working on my next one. On top of the books, my podcast, and whatever TV I do, I will always write stand-up because I love it the most. And why wouldn't I? If you approach it the way I do, stand-up is a gamble and a thrill ride every time.

Stand-up is also the only risk I'm paid to take. At this point in my life, I get up there and I've got nothing to prove. I've lived through enough crazy shit that even if I were a dimwit comic, I could get on stage and entertain people just by telling stories for a few minutes. Doing it well is a gift, because being funny is a very powerful thing. In social circles, the funniest person commands the room. It isn't the richest man or the best-looking woman; it's the funniest person who has control over everyone. If you can make people laugh, you can make people listen to you. If you are truly funny, you will end up at the front of the line. People like being around funny people, because humor makes everyone feel smarter and more alive.

As a comic, when we get onstage, it's an acknowledgment from the world that we are so funny and so interesting that people who don't even know us are willing to pay money to hear what we have to say. Think about that for a moment. We do; and that's why once we have fans, we feel the pressure to always be good and to keep getting better. Fans are invaluable to a comic because they both encourage and challenge us. Good audiences at a comedy club have an energy that we can feel.

"Okay, motherfucker. So you think you're funny? Well, be funny. Show me what you've got."

That's the attitude of a good audience, and that vibe that feeds us. Doing stand-up is walking a tightrope strung up by your ego, and every joke that works is one step farther across the abyss of your insecurity and self-loathing. When you get the balance right, you're invincible. I've slept with women so far out of my league because they'd just seen me kill. That kind of success is immediate power. If I bomb, the same woman will never fuck me, because even if she sees me kill the very next night, the stench of failure will always be on me. If everything goes right, I'm Warren Beatty in the '70s; if it doesn't, I'm a midget with syphilis.

I love offending people. I love wandering out there on the edge because I love chance. I love bets where the odds are fifty-fifty, like telling a joke with no clue as to how the audience will react. When I do that, I'm proud, because it reminds me of why I'm doing this in the first place. It reminds me of the first time I heard a Richard Pryor album. Pryor did not give a fuck, ever. He talked about everything that people were scared of at the time: racism, drug use, and police oppression. That was forty years ago, by the way, which says a lot about how much we've grown as a society. Pryor was, to say the least, ahead of his time.

He talked about those aspects of our society in a way that was so raw that I felt like I'd get arrested just for listening to him.

That is what comedy should be like. Comics should speak the truth while offending every single person in sight. If you don't believe me, here's an example. In 2004, I was playing the Aspen Laff Festival, and at the time, I was still very much off the wagon. I did a set at 1:00 a.m., and at that hour, a festival crowd is the real deal: comedy writers, comics, and agents. At the time, my manager (who is no longer my manager but not because of anything that happened that night) was trying to close a deal for me to do a comedy special with HBO. There were a lot of influential people from the network there, including Michael Patrick King, the executive producer, writer, and figurehead of *Sex and the City*. Whatever you might think of that show, it was an HBO institution and in 2004 was in the midst of a popular and successful final season after six years. My former manager knew that Michael Patrick King was in the audience and told me to tone it down and play it safe. His reasoning was that we were on the verge of selling the special and that I could do whatever I wanted to after that, but until then I should keep it on the level.

As an extremely heterosexual former longshoreman from New Jersey, even I knew that *Sex and the City* was written by the gayest men alive, so I did a set that revolved around one question: Am I homophobic?

I haven't done it in a while, but it's an extended bit where I psychoanalyze myself in front of the audience, playing both a therapist and myself, each of us trying to figure out if I'm homophobic or not. It's a showcase for my most homophobic material, and on this particular night, I found a way to work in not only my stuff but every good gay joke I've ever heard. I destroyed, as I do whenever I pull this routine out. Michael Patrick King and his entourage of *Sex and the City* writers walked out in the middle of it, which I took as a badge of honor. I was glad they didn't like me; some people can be so arrogant about comedy. Anyway, their exit sent my set into flux for a minute, because everyone who had been laughing at the gay jokes suddenly wondered if they'd been wrong to do so, but I won them back pretty quickly. A lot of gay guys who have heard me do that bit think it's hilarious for the same reason the *Sex and the City* crew did not: they like it because it's rude, crude, and not socially acceptable. We all have preferences and peccadilloes that we'd prefer to keep private, but dragging them out into the light of day is fucking funny. That is your job as a comic: to talk about shit that most people don't want to talk about.

The mood in the green room after my set was pretty uncomfortable. The two comics who had opened for me were there hanging out, and they were politically correct women who were hoping to get into HBO's good graces. Sarah Jessica Parker popped in to say hello to one of them and ignored me, the three-hundred-pound baby gorilla in the room. My fondest memory of that night is my former manager trying to be upbeat.

"Art, it's going to be a lot harder for me to sell them a special after that walkout, but I'll do my best."

He thought my career was over.

Which is why he's no longer my manager: he was wrong. The next day, HBO called his office and offered me $250,000 for a one-hour comedy special. The next week, *The Onion* ran a front-page story with a picture of me and the greatest headline I've ever seen: FCC SENTENCES ARTIE LANGE TO DEATH. These two career highlights were achieved because I listened to no one else but me that night.

That is why I never shy away from a gay joke when the most important gays in the world are in the audience. The lesson to learn here is that whoever you are and whatever you do, don't ever be afraid to go for broke. There is no tried-and-true set of rules to this thing we call life, so go with your gut and play to win. If you don't, you're a fag.

10

OFF-CAMPUS BETTING

The most illegal enterprise I've ever been a part of took place at a diner with a business model that I can't believe hasn't spread like a California wildfire. It was a diner with a strip club attached to it. What could be better than a cheeseburger after a lap dance? What was even better was that if you spent money at the strip club, the bill you got was a check from the diner. I remember going through my tax receipts with my accountant and him looking up from the papers, totally confused, asking how I managed to spend $5,000 in one night at a diner.

"Well, let's see. I remember I had the special, the Puerto Rican omelet, which was expensive because it had two big yolks. I'm talking farm-raised, imported, extra-large yolks."

To tell you the truth, the yolk was on me, because for the same $5,000, I could have gotten four hundred blow jobs and a pizza with two toppings ten feet outside of the Holland Tunnel.

Illegal activity was an accepted feature of how the long-shoremen ran the ports in New York and New Jersey from the 1950s all the way through the '80s. But by the end of the '80s, it had gotten so out of hand with goods falling off trucks, entire containers going missing, and drugs being moved that something had to be done. The union had to maintain the respect and cooperation of the management companies that ran the warehouses, so they cracked down on the criminality and stopped turning a blind eye. It was a major transformation, and the guy who got me the job was a tremendously influential figure in that change. This coincided with a reorganization of the port system in the New York area. Hell's Kitchen in western Manhattan had always been ground zero for ships unloading their containers, but in the '80s, that port was closed, redirecting an enormous amount of traffic to Red Hook, Brooklyn, and two ports in New Jersey: Bayonne and Newark, where I worked.

By the time I started in 1991, everything was legit, with the union acting as an enforcement agency as much as it was an advocate for our rights as workers. If you were caught stealing, the union would discharge you for misconduct immediately. Of course, guys still found ways to get away with it, but it was a riskier proposition than it once was. In other words, there was more action. The bookies still took bets from us like they had always done, but it wasn't on-site or out in the open anymore. It was called "off-campus betting," because no one did it on union ground or on union phones. There was a network that made it happen, which I hooked into pretty quickly, and that's how I landed the most dangerous job I've ever had. Despite the fact that it was a fast track to serious jail time, it was one hell of a side gig.

The reason why we didn't place bets on the pay phones at the port was because all the calls were logged. So off-campus bettors used the phones at bars or restaurants close by and placed bets on their lunch hour, which is how I discovered my favorite diner. I'd go there and call my bookie, Bobo, who is the guy I've always bet with, even when I lived in LA. It probably sounds crazy that I used a bookie on Staten Island when I lived 2,500 miles away, but when you hear the rest of this story, you'll understand. Our relationship went on for years, and for obvious reasons, I was afraid to say Bobo's name on the air when I was at *Stern*, but he has since disappeared and it's been a while now, so I think it's finally safe for me to talk about him. Actually, he's dead, so I've got the all clear.

Now I'm no gangster, but it was obvious to me that a lot of the regulars at the diner weren't the type who paid all their taxes, if you know what I mean. It was normal to see a guy come in, sit down in a booth with another guy, and say something like, "Can you believe it? Two fucking niggers stole the truck we lifted last night." If the owner of the diner got 0.1 percent of the profits of every deal arranged on that phone, his diner/strip club chain would have gone national within a year. The diner has a different name now, but it's still there, by the way. I bet that the former owner is either under indictment or in witness protection, working at a Cinnabon in Iowa.

So one day I was in the diner placing bets and having lunch when a guy came up to me and asked if I worked at the car pier.

"No," I said. "Orange juice."

"Good. Listen, I've got a job for you, and it's easy money."

"Oh yeah?"

"Yeah. You'll make a phone call from that pay phone that you're on all the time and you'll give a guy some information, and I'll pay you cash. Easy."

In the 1990s, Newark was a hot spot for car theft, because it was where supply and demand came together. The freight ships stacked with containers full of cars from Japan and Europe were so huge that they'd block out the sun when they pulled into the port. There was so much volume that when things went missing, it was just par for the course, and there were chop shops all over Newark, because everyone was ripping off cars. They were being jacked in broad daylight at busy intersections with entire families in them. The thieves weren't only looking for luxury cars, either; they were taking anything with wheels and selling it whole or in parts. If you drove through downtown Newark at all after dark, there was a good chance you'd end up walking home.

It was such a problem by 1990 that New Jersey passed legislature making carjacking a crime punishable by up to thirty years in prison. That put a lot of guys away, but it didn't put a dent in the larger operation at work. The goodfella who approached me had a very organized system. He had a team of thieves who stole the cars and other guys who picked them up from prearranged locations and took them to his chop shops. I never saw this, but I'm guessing that his crew then stripped them down and sold the parts or sawed off the VIN numbers and sold the entire car to vendors overseas. I played a very small role in this enterprise. All that he asked me to do was call the thieves who were going to pick up the cars and give them the location of the pickup. That seems like something that no one would need to pay a jerk-off like me a few thousand bucks to do. But a lot of guys in his line of work didn't like to make calls that could implicate them, which would happen if the cops or feds had tapped the phone of the guy on the other end. They needed someone unconnected to them to be their secretary.

I'd set up shop in the booth next to the pay phone, three days a week. You were allowed to smoke in restaurants back then, so I'd sit, have lunch, smoke, and answer the phone when it rang. The voice on the other end would give me a password, a phone number, a time, a location, and instructions about where to find the keys, and since I wasn't allowed to write anything down besides the phone number, I had to memorize it all. I've always been good at memorization, so that part was easy. If you don't believe me, I'll bet whatever is in your checking account that I can recite your favorite scene from *The Godfather* verbatim. I did that for Francis Ford Coppola, and even he couldn't believe that I didn't miss the name of one capo in the speech that Michael gives when he sends Carlo to Vegas.

"Every don and in the right order too," he said. "Nobody ever gets Stracci."

Anyway, back at the diner, once I'd gotten the information, I'd place the call, and after the guy who answered gave me the password, I'd give him the address and tell him where to find the keys. The instructions were always very specific, like, "Leave the keys under the yellow cone stapled to the dirt by the construction site halfway down the block," or "Look under the right side of the Dumpster with the Dunkin' Donuts sign on the side." Once a car was safely delivered to wherever it was going, I'd be paid $1,500 per car.

The guy who was paying me had clearly done time or done enough crime to worry about being under surveillance by the feds, but that didn't bother me. I told myself that I wasn't putting my job at the port at risk because I wasn't doing any business there, so this off-campus side hustle was worth it. By that point in my life, I had a lot of disorderly conduct charges and bar fights on my record but no grade-A felonies, so if I got caught, I wouldn't be going to jail for long. And that would only happen if I called someone whose phone was tapped. I was okay with those odds for $1,500 a phone call.

In 1991, I was twenty-three years old, and I made $70,000 at the port, because I put in my eight hundred hours and qualified for the container check, which was $5,000. That same year, off-campus I made $90,000. I had no idea what to do with all that cash, and I had no one to ask, so I told my accountant. He made me pay taxes on it, because that, he said, is how the government always gets you. Here are a few examples: Al Capone, Martha Stewart, and Wesley Snipes. So I did the smart thing and gave Uncle Sam his cut of my $90,000, claiming I'd earned it doing bodyguard work for an older business owner who deposited his payroll checks late at night. It was a likely story, because in Newark, longshoremen were hired for work like that all the time.

I was heading down a bad road and making too much money, but I didn't feel guilty about it. No one was getting hurt, and who were we ripping off? BMW? Insurance companies? Sure, consumers end up paying more to cover the manufacturers' losses, but so what? I loved the excitement, I loved sitting there in the diner, shooing away anyone who wanted to use the phone, acting like it was my personal business line. The guy I was working for had juice with the owner, so I could do as I pleased. The danger of doing something illegal thrilled me and made my life at the port worth living. I loved the action, I loved the money, and I loved feeling like a gangster. Even after taxes I had so much cash that that I had no idea where to put it. I stuffed it under my mattress, I stashed it in shoe boxes at the top of my closet, I put it anywhere I could think of. My mother is smart, so she knew that something was up, because no one makes $160,000 a year loading trucks at the port, even if they're given a plum gig like mine. She never said it, but I think that played a role in her decision to allow me to leave the port and try comedy again. I bet she suspected that I was involved in something that was going to end a lot worse than my last open mic appearance.

With her permission, I slowly decreased my hours at the port, got a job as a cab driver, and started taking the cab into the city during my night shifts to do a few minutes on any stage that would have me. My buddy Sal Santoro and his father worked at the cab company, and I used to drop by to visit them so I could grab a slice at a pizza place across the street that I liked. I'd hang out and tell all the drivers how I was going to be a comedian. An old German guy named Cliff owned the operation, and since I could spell my name, he knew that I was qualified to join the team. It was astounding how many idiots worked there.

Most of them were examples of what happens to burnouts in high school after high school, when they have more time on their hands to get burned out. Cliff's interview consisted of this:

"So do you know where Row Avenue is?" he asked.

"Yeah."

"You're hired; you know more than half of my employees."

Cliff was very understanding and let me make my own hours, so I worked nights and it was the perfect job. Drivers kept 35 percent of their fares and their tips, so if I made $500 during a shift, I'd keep $175 plus tips, which would usually add up to about $250 on a good night. It was enough to cover my monthly nut, and if it was a good month, I'd be able to give my mother some spending money and still have enough left over for bus fare to New York and beer money on the nights I didn't drive there in the cab. Most of the time, I'd even have enough extra to crash at a cheap hotel in the city if I wanted to.

For two weeks I also had a job as a waiter. Here's how well that went: The night before I had to work my first brunch I got stop-signed by a bouncer at the Rusty Scupper in West Orange, and the next morning my nose started bleeding while I took an order. The yuppies at the table started screaming, and my manager fired me on the spot. The manager was also a friend of my sister's, and she was so mad at me when I told her that he let me go.

"What happened?" she asked.

"Nothing. They just didn't need me anymore."

"That's bullshit, Art. You did something. I begged him to hire you."

"Yeah, I know. I guess he overestimated how many

people he needed for brunch. Plus, I didn't really fit in. I'm not much of a brunch guy."

"Fuck you, Artie. I'm going to call my friend and apologize for wasting his time."

"Hey, Stacey?"

"What?"

"When you talk to him, can you ask him for the eight dollars they owe me?"

But before I embarked on this new phase of gainful employment, I had to have a conversation with my off-campus employer, because, unlike a brunch shift, a car-theft ring wasn't a vocation you simply walked away from. Most guys, in fact, never leave a situation like that unless they're killed or locked up, so I had to do a big song and dance about how I wasn't going to say anything. It took quite a while to assure him that he could trust me and that I wasn't a rat.

He stared at me long and hard and then asked, "So what are you doing now if you're not working at the port and you're not working for me?"

"I'm trying to be a comedian," I said.

"Sure you are. What are you really doing?"

"No, I mean it. I'm trying to be a comedian. I know it's a risk, but I have to try it."

"What do you mean, you have to try it?"

I had no answer to that, so I just said, "Yeah."

"So you're trying to be like who? James Caan?"

I thought he was kidding until I realized that James Caan was the only comparison he could draw.

"Yeah, exactly like that. If I end up just like James Caan, that would be great. Honestly, that's what I'm hoping for."

Forget James Caan. At this point in my career, being

like Scott Caan would be great. Madeline Kahn, Sammy Cahn, I'd take any Caan and be happy with it. So after he was absolutely sure that I wasn't lying, the guy let me go, with one condition: that I continued to bet with Bobo, who was a part of his extended crime family. He said he'd feel better about letting me go if he knew how to find me, wherever I was. Clearly, he knew how to read people, because he could tell that I would be betting on sports for years to come.

The truth is that my off-campus job satisfied me on two levels, and for a while I thought about continuing it, even though I knew I shouldn't. It provided me with a financial cushion that working as a cabbie never would. When that money started to wear thin, there were a few times I almost made the long drive to the port to ask for my job back, and that is when I regretted getting out of the car racket the most. But more than the money, it gave me the rush and the risk fix that every degenerate gambler craves. It was the ideal job, because it provided both the edge that I yearned for and the money that I required for betting. The port was an interesting place to me, because it was full of characters, but at the end of the day, I went to the same place and did the same thing day in and day out. I loaded trucks; there was no change and no excitement, whereas my off-campus job supplied plenty of both.

Luckily, even though it started slowly, show business started to give me the buzz I needed. Show business does that, and if you approach it recklessly like I did, it can provide years of thrills! To tell you the truth, that's why I enjoy my one-off comedy shows more than I do my larger, regular gigs at places like the Borgata. When I do a one-off right, I feel like the Jesse James of dick jokes. I show up, I do my act, and I get the fuck out of there with the money like I just robbed the place. I can't explain how much I love that feeling. As I'm pulling away, I feel like I've just won that money, even though I know it's not true. I love anything that makes me feel like I've won money, because winning it is so much better than earning it. When I win money, I feel like I'm getting one over on the world. It makes me feel like I'm not a sucker.

The car theft ring gave me that same rush, which is how I know that if I didn't end up onstage for a living, I would have continued on with it and gotten into real trouble. Instead, three years later, I went to LA to start my television career, and after that imploded, I came back and landed my job at *Stern*.

Around that time is also when I founded something I call "the Bank of Artie." Even with my gambling losses and drug habits, I was making good money, some of which I dedicated to supporting four or five friends of mine who can't take care of themselves. I started paying their rent, the way I still do for Dan the Bad Cop, and for most of them still, if I'm being honest. These guys are dear friends, and they'd all be in homeless shelters if I didn't provide them with somewhere to live. It's not a ton of money, but for different reasons, they need every bit they can get. Some have been through bad divorces; others have crippling medical bills or can't get steady work because they've served time. I got lured into helping them because when it starts it's always supposed to be temporary, but at this point it's not.

It's what I do instead of giving money to charity, because they are my philanthropy. Unfortunately this kind of giving isn't tax deductable.

All of them go to my business manager and pick up their checks at the beginning of the month, and all of them always tell me they'll pay me back someday. If they do, fantastic. They're all great guys that I'm happy to help out, because they've given up on their manhood, but a couple of them have taken advantage for a bit too long now. They simply don't care to try to get out of their situation, because they have good credit at the Bank of Artie. I've asked one or two of them if they've ever felt bad about taking my hard-earned cash. Each of them said the same thing.

"No. Why would I?"

One guy even asked me for a check for two grand one day, and as I sat there filling it out with a disgusted look on my face, he said, "Hey, man, what's with the attitude?" Unbelievable.

Not too long ago, after I was under indictment for an arrest following a bender, a different one of the guys whose rent I pay came to see me. He was in trouble for something—he didn't say for what or how—he just told me he needed money . . . a lot of money. That was the last straw: I told him I wouldn't do it and couldn't help him at all anymore. By my estimation, he was into me for $200,000 in rent over the years. I stood up to him so he would learn to stand up for himself.

"Well, it's hard for me to get a job that makes any good money, man," he said. "And I need money fast. How about that car thing you used to do?"

"What are you talking about?"

"That old thing you used to do, the thing with the guy with the guys?"

"The guy with the guys?"

"The guy with the cars? With the guys who took the cars?" he said.

"Oh! The guy with the cars. The off-campus guy?"

"Yeah."

Back in the day, I made the mistake of mentioning my other job to one or two buddies. I did it because I knew they had cars they wanted to "sell," and if I brought cars in, I got a bigger kickback. Once I knew what my friend was talking about, he asked if I could get in touch with the guy who did the thing with the guys and the cars, off-campus. He wanted me to make an introduction.

The smart thing to do would have been to give my friend some money and send him packing. Instead, I decided to call a guy who knew the guy who did the thing with the cars. It had been a while, but I still knew the guy to call to get the number of the other guy. I wasn't even sure if the guy I knew could connect me with the guy who did the thing with the cars, because that guy had "gone away to college," which is what they say when guys like that go to prison. From what I'd heard, he'd done a two-year degree at junior college but behaved in art class, so he got his diploma early, if you know what I mean.

Anyway, I called him, and he was out of the game, but I got the number of another guy who I'd met off-campus years ago. I called him and was told that none of the guys I used to know were doing the thing with the cars anymore.

"So what are you asking me?" he asked.

"You know what I'm asking," I said. "My friend has a bad transmission."

"Okay."

"He's looking to get it fixed. Do you still bank at the same corner?" I asked.

"What corner?"

"The corner. The same corner."

"Nope, I don't bank anywhere in the city anymore . . . *because I stopped banking.*"

"Oh, really? Okay, good. Thanks."

I told my dependent that I'd made the call and it was a no-go and that I couldn't help him. And what did he do? He went to his uncle for the money and got it without question. He'd had that option available the whole time; he just wanted to see what kind of loan he could get at the Bank of Artie. This happens to athletes, famous people, and lottery winners every single day.

His greed taught me a lesson because rather than say no or give him some fuck-off money, I chose the dumbest option and made the call. It was the riskiest way I could have helped him. Considering my numerous mistakes, mishaps, and brushes with the law in the past few years, did I really need to call a known member of an organized crime ring? No, I didn't. And this is why I'm a loser: *because I loved it.*

I felt like I was in it again. I was the guy on the phone, doing something illegal. I was the guy who beat the system, and I felt like I'd just won money. I'd missed those loser thrills.

Since the day I walked out of that diner for the last time in 1992, I've been on a sketch comedy show and a network sitcom, I've made movies that *Vanity Fair* calls cult classics.

I cohosted *The Howard Stern Show* for a decade, I've had a number-one *New York Times* bestseller, I've toured the country and Afghanistan. I have a thank-you letter from the USO in my office. The owner of the Patriots sent a private jet for me so that I could be paid handsomely to do a private show for his kid's birthday. I've had sex with women way, way out of my league, including eleven strippers in a week. I have managed not to die from my excesses, and I've managed to live almost every one of my dreams. Sure, I've lost a lot of money, and even though celebritynetworth.com is wrong in saying that I have $10 million because they aren't counting the times the Broncos didn't cover or the $40,000 that walked out of here on my ex-fiancée's finger, I'm still in the black. Listen, if they say I'm worth ten million, that means I've made twenty million in order to have ten, even if I don't have it anymore. What I'm trying to say is that however you slice it, at this point I'm still doing well, and I'm on the verge of doing even better.

I had no reason to make that phone call, but still . . . I did it. And after that fleeting thrill was gone, I forgot all about it.

Which brings me to a night a few months later, when I went out for a drive and found myself surrounded by what seemed like a SWAT team. Where I live in Hoboken is pretty quiet and residential, so this was very out of the ordinary. I was still under indictment, so my first thought was that I was fucked and going to the big house for a while, even though I had no idea what I'd done. I mean, there were things that I'd done, so I thought this was about that, but it wasn't. This was about the guy who did the thing with the cars. The guy I'd spoken to had been talking slowly and asking questions for a reason: his knew his phone was tapped. I replayed the conversation in my head.

"Hey, it's Artie. Do you remember me?"

"Artie? Artie who? I don't know any Arties."

"It's Artie Lange. You don't remember?"

"Artie . . . Artie Lange, you said?"

"Yeah, Artie Lange."

"Artie Lange . . . Artie Lange . . . yeah, I think I remember you. How you doin'?"

He said my first and last name about five times during the call. The cops said that that when they heard my name on the tape, they couldn't believe it. Since I was under indictment, pursuing criminal activity carried a potential sentence of ten years. They had every right to throw the book at me too, because I was blatant about asking the guy if he was still stealing cars. This was a bad situation, so I pulled my one and only get-out-of-jail-free card. When they took me down to the precinct, I called an influential member of law enforcement that I know and explained my predicament. About five hours later, I was released with no charges. I don't know exactly what happened, but something did. What I do know is that ever since, I've really enjoyed every benefit appearance I've done for the police. I've logged so many of them this past year that they're honoring me at the New Jersey Blue Lives Matter event, and I can't wait for that either.

It was a close call, but that's how much of a loser I am. I put my role on Judd Apatow's show *Crashing* and my slot on a monthlong comedy tour with Judd and Pete Holmes to publicize the show (where we would travel entirely by private jet, by the way) at risk for a guy who had been living off me for years. I can't explain why I made that call so easily other than admitting that it satisfied the evil in me. When I played the call back in my head, I realized how the guy had backtracked and led me down the path. But what I realized more is how much he didn't have to, because I was the one pushing; I was the one actively trying to commit a crime, not him. He said no, but I kept at it, asking him if he knew someone else I could call. He kept refusing, but that didn't stop me, because being in that dangerous, illegal situation gave me a thrill and filled the void in me, and I wanted to enjoy it for a little while.

When I was in the jail cell, playing 500 Rummy with a few of the older detectives, I thought, *This isn't bad at all. I'm back here doing this. I'm back in Loser Land and it's great! This life is uncomplicated, and fuck it, I'm happy.*

You don't have to say it, I'll say it for you: there is something very wrong with me, and here's why. If I had a wife and two kids, I wouldn't have done anything differently, and that's because I have no shame. When I'm bored to death, I'll do whatever it takes to alleviate my boredom. In this case, I even threw some denial on top, telling myself I was just trying to help a friend. Not at all. I didn't make that call for him. I wanted a taste of the illicit rush I get from fucking up.

11

DIRTY WORK

One of my favorite people on earth is Norm Macdonald. Not only is he a smart and funny motherfucker, he's also a degenerate gambler. He and I share the same primal need for action, but to tell you the truth, since his bankroll is much, much fatter than mine, Norm is even worse than I am. I love him so much, and I think the feeling is mutual, but I know he will agree with me when I say that we are terrible for each other.

Norm and I first met in 1997, when he offered me a costarring role in *Dirty Work*. It's a buddy comedy directed by Bob Saget, with Norm playing the lead role and me playing his fat sidekick. I wasn't the only guy up for the role, but Norm liked the sketch comedy work I'd done on *Mad TV* and thought we'd be a good fit. He was right about that in more ways than one. This was the first role in a major motion picture that I'd ever landed, and at the time, I'd been fired from *Mad TV* for drugs and bad behavior, so

Norm was really taking a chance on me. He believed in me, so much so that he had to convince the producers and a handful of studio executives that I was worth it.

Making movies is like going to summer camp: everyone on the production is stuck in a bubble far away from home, so even if you don't like your fellow cast members, you have to find a way to get along. We shot in Toronto, and the first night, Norm, Saget, a few others, and I went out to a bar. We drank and played pool, and I introduced Norm to nine-ball, or cutthroat as some like to call it. Naturally we played for money, and I ended up taking Norm for $2,000. My manager at the time, who'd had to vouch for me a thousand different ways to get me the job, nearly had a heart attack when he heard about it.

"Why the hell would you do that on the first night? Couldn't you have lost to him?"

Norm, however, was an honorable guy and even did the culturally appropriate thing by paying me in Canadian dollars. He explained that $2,000 Canadian was a lot less than $2,000 US, but that was the price I had to pay since I'd won the bet in Canada. He didn't give me an accurate idea of the exchange rate, unfortunately. If I'd known that the US dollar was worth more than the Canadian dollar at the time, I wouldn't have given a stripper my pocketful of Canadian cash, thinking it was worth half. The next day I learned that I'd paid her the equivalent of $3,000 US for a blow job. Needless to say, it was the beginning of a beautiful friendship between Norm and me.

Dirty Work was the best summer camp I've ever been to. We had so much fun, and it was structured perfectly, with all the famous actors playing supporting roles and doing cameos coming up for a week at a time. It was nonstop excitement because so many of my and Norm's heroes had been cast. I got to know Jack Ward, Adam Sandler, and Chris Farley in a way that I never would have if we hadn't been in that movie bubble together. I am especially grateful that I got to spend some real time with Chris, who made a tremendous impression on me and who I wish were still with us.

I'm going to share a Farley story now that I've never really told before, because why not? When we wrapped *Dirty Work* in October of 1997, Norm returned to New York to begin the next season of *Saturday Night Live* and invited me to come down not long after that. Farley, who had been fired from *SNL* in 1995, was hosting, and Norm wanted me to be there to help keep an eye on him for the week. This was a ridiculous plan, because not only did I look up to Farley, but by then, I liked partying almost as much as he did. Nevertheless, Norm was worried about Chris, and since he wasn't the type to organize an intervention, to Norm, having me around Chris was his way of looking out for his friend. Being such a huge fan of Farley's, I gladly signed up for duty.

Farley—and this is coming from me—was completely out of his mind. He was staying at the Waldorf Astoria and running through hookers and blow like there was no tomorrow. He was lonely, he was tired, he was at the end of his rope. After *SNL*, he'd gone to LA and he'd made a bunch of movies, and he told story after story about how everyone who had gotten close to him used him for one thing or another. It was truly heartbreaking. At that point he was hiring hookers to come to his room just to talk to him. I didn't understand that at the time, but I do now.

Chris made it through the week; he was a great host and a true professional, despite how he was living off-camera. Every Saturday, it's a tradition that after the episode airs, there's a wrap party, and that week, Norm, Chris, and I all went together. Norm was doing his best to look out for Chris because he was worried, and had reason to be, but when someone doesn't want help, there isn't much you can do. At one point in the party, Norm went outside to take a phone call and asked me to keep an eye on Farley. Andy Dick was there that night, and he and Chris were running around, and while Norm was away, I watched them both go into the bathroom together. There are only two reasons why a guy goes into a bathroom with Andy Dick, and neither of them are squeaky clean.

"Hey, man, how's Farley?" Norm asked when he returned.

"I don't know, man. He was doing all right, but I just saw him go into the men's room with Andy Dick."

"Oh my God," Norm said. "I hope he's getting high."

Three weeks later, on December 18, Chris died. *Dirty Work* was my first film and his last. The next five movies I did—*Lost & Found*, *Mystery Men*, *The 4th Floor*, *The Bachelor*, and *Puppet*—all tanked. I wasn't the lead in any of them, but I felt those failures as if I were. To me, it was a sign that I was more of a small-screen guy, so I decided to focus on television and forget about my big-screen aspirations. Norm had his own sitcom on ABC, and since we had such great chemistry in *Dirty Work*, I got cast as his fat sidekick once again. The show was perfect for him: he played an ex-hockey player, which appealed to his Canadian roots, who had gotten kicked out of the league for gambling, which meant he didn't need to stretch as an actor. Working on *The Norm Show* was the easiest money I've ever made. We did twenty-two episodes a year, and for the two years I was on it, I made $35,000 a week. It was winning the lottery for me, because I'd come from the sketch comedy world, where, even on a show like *SNL*, you make a lot less and do a lot more work. Why do you think every cast member on that show jumps at the first chance they get to star in a movie or a sitcom, even if it's not that good?

My job on *Norm* consisted of two to three lines an episode. For example, I'd be in a scene with Norm, and I'd say something like, "Are you thinking what I'm thinking?" And Norm would say something like, "No, I'm not thinking about cheeseburgers." I'd give Norm or the camera a goofy look, they'd add canned laughter in postproduction, and that would be my big scene for the week. I got in a lot of trouble for going on *Conan O'Brien* during that time and being honest with him about how easy it was.

"Do you like being on a sitcom?" Conan asked.

"Are you kidding me? I love it!" I said. "I do a couple of lines a week and on Friday I get a check for thirty-five grand!"

That got huge laughs, but one of the executive producers of *Norm* who wasn't very fond of me called me and ripped me a new one. He wasn't mad that I'd been such a wiseass; the problem was that I was making twice as much as some of the other cast members who were doing twice the work I was. Rightfully so, he didn't want me rubbing that fact in anyone's face. My salary had nothing to do with me being friends with Norm, by the way. I had been a leading cast member on *Mad TV* for two years; plus my handful of film credits, successful or not, helped boost my value. Plus, I was represented by the William Morris Agency, which had a lot of pull and negotiated a great rate for me. At the time, I didn't see what the problem was. If anything, I was being honest, and isn't honesty the best policy?

During the two years we worked together on *The Norm Show*, Norm and I gambled on everything, every week, every day. We never did the obvious, like the football pool at the office. That's gambling for people who don't gamble, and we had zero interest in amateur bullshit. Even if you went 15–1 in the office pool, you'd only win something like thirty-eight bucks. Let's say I had that great of a season, how could I even pretend to be happy knowing that if I'd placed the same bets in Vegas I'd have four hundred thousand instead of thirty-eight bucks in my pocket?

We had no interest in betting with the writers, producers, or anyone else because we were too busy chasing our own action, and we never invited any of those people to join us. Norm and I declined all the office pools, but we used to send an intern to Vegas to place our bets. We recruited a kid from Iowa who had just graduated from UCLA and had never placed a bet in his life. He was so out of his element; we'd put him in a rental car with $50,000 in cash and send him to the Race and Sports Book at the Mirage with a list of bets. He was scared to death of us. We did that to him at least two or three times.

Unlike me, Norm didn't like betting with bookies. I understood why; he'd been burned badly a few times, and the biggest of them was my fault. Back in New York, when he was still on *SNL*, Norm needed a bookie and asked me if I had one. By this page in the book, you all know that I had Bobo, so I set him up. Betting with a bookie is dangerous, because you can bet on credit, and if you get ahead of yourself and can't pay up, you get your legs broken. In Vegas, if you want to place a bet for $10,000, you have to show up with $10,000. If you bet with a bookie, it's a phone call, so it doesn't seem real. Before you know it, if things don't go your way, you owe someone $20,000, and it's a pretty terrible feeling. One minute you're screaming your head off watching whatever game you've bet on, and the next, if things don't go your way, you're in deep shit. You now owe money to somebody dangerous, which leaves you stuck thinking about all the work you had to do to earn the money you just lost and how much more work you'll have to do to pay off your debt. If you start betting with a bookie regularly, you either need a big bankroll or a lot of restraint, because things can snowball in a hurry.

When it comes to sports betting, the highest high is a lightning bet. Say you bet the over/under on a basketball game and the magic number is 180 points. If you bet the over, you are wagering that the combined score of both teams will be greater than 180. If you bet the under, you're betting that fewer than 180 points will be scored in the game. Generally, I like to bet the over, because if a score ends in a tie and goes into overtime, you're almost guaranteed to hit the over. Games played by equally matched, low-scoring teams, also known as defensive matchups, are contests that you might consider betting the under. But I don't like to do that, because those games are also likely to go into overtime, and overtime is death to under bets.

I hate betting the under, because there's no fun in it. I don't see the point. Betting the over is so much more exciting, because you're rooting for both teams to score. You're rooting for fireworks; you're rooting for action. The over is also better, because it's the only bet you can win before the game is finished. The added bonus of betting the over is that usually you confuse the people around you by cheering for both teams and celebrating every time a point is scored. You'll cheer for one team, and if they throw an interception, you start shouting for the other team to score. It's nonstop thrills! If you bet the over, your favorite team is whichever one has the ball.

A lightning bet is an additional wager on every point scored over the over or under the under. Here's how that works. Let's say you take the over on a college basketball game and add a lightning bet of $100: once the teams go over the magic number, you get $100 for every point scored. Every basket after that is $200, every three-pointer is $300. If the game goes into overtime and you get twenty points in excess of the over, that's $2,000. That's a very nice win on a basketball game. That's the kind of action I'd take, but Norm would bet ten times that. If I bet the over with $100 on a lightning bet, he'd bet the over with $1,000 on a lightning bet—the pinnacle of degenerate gambling.

When you hit, a lightning bet is great, but if you don't, it can put a real hurt on you. If you don't cover the number, meaning the combined score falls short of the over, you pay for every point it's short by. One or two points will piss you off, but if it gets into double digits, you're taking a huge loss. When you've got a lightning bet going, most of the game is brutal to watch. You want both teams to score as much as possible, so three-pointers are great but free throws are the best because the score goes up while the clock is stopped. In the last quarter, as the score inches closer to the over, the excitement ramps up to where you can barely take it. You're watching the clock, you're watching the game, and anticipation has complete control of you. Once you hit your number, that's it, you're high, riding a wave of pure adrenaline because every single basket until time runs out is money in your pocket. There's nothing like it; you're cheering for every single score and you start to feel like the players are playing just for you. Your heart pounds, you're light-headed—it's insanity. It's luck, it's the rush, it's pure unadulterated gambling.

The only thing better than placing lightning bets alone is doing it with a friend. When the two of you are rooting for the same outcome, there's nothing better. There is always some asshole rooting for the other team at whatever sports bar or casino you go to, but if you've placed a lightning bet, they can't piss you off anymore. It's impossible, because you're winning as long as somebody is scoring. Being that kind of fan next to people taking the game seriously is a foolproof way to have a blast while pissing people off.

Norm and I loved lightning bets. I opened for him on a stand-up tour between seasons of the show, and every night, we'd pick a game and put some action on a lightning bet. We'd bet on college hoops, college football, and pro basketball and watch the games at the nearest bar we could find and scream like maniacs. We had the most luck with college hoops, but sometimes we'd catch a break on a college football game. The pros usually let us down.

We bottomed out on June 7, 1998, when the Utah Jazz set a record for futility versus the Chicago Bulls in game 3 of the NBA Finals. Michael Jordan and the Bulls held the Jazz to just fifty-four points. The Jazz was a low-scoring team at the time, but fifty-four points was still thirty points below their average. I lost $18,000 on that game, which still bothers me, while Norm lost $105,000. Neither of us has forgiven John Stockton or Karl Malone for serving up utter shit on a stick that night.

Here's the thing about gambling: even though we know that luck comes in runs, a degenerate gambler remains in the game no matter what. Which is why the Jazz set Norm off on a loss run of $100,000 a week for three weeks running. Norm's credit with the bookie was great; he could bet as often and as much as he wanted, and he loved that. But once he was $100,000 in the hole, they came to collect. I went to *SNL* with the bookie the first time they did so. Norm gave him $105,000 in a brown paper shopping bag, which the bookie and I walked down Sixth Avenue back to his car on that sunny Tuesday afternoon.

Eventually, Norm turned his luck around and won $100,000 in a week, and when he did, he sent me to collect. I set up a meeting, but the guy didn't show up. I called and called, but he never answered. I didn't panic, because bookies don't operate like normal businesses. They're illegal, so they don't have offices, they aren't in the yellow pages, and they're constantly moving their operations and changing their phone numbers to stay one step ahead of the law. I didn't freak out when I couldn't get through to the guy, because it was par for the course. I figured that something must have happened and that I'd hear from him in a day or so, because when bookies change their numbers, they always reach out to their customers to let them know, because it's the only way they make money.

The bookie never called, and once the evening games started a day later, I knew that he had disappeared owing Norm $100,000. I did not look forward to telling Norm that after three straight weeks of paying, the guy had taken a powder and was never going to show up with his money.

I went to tell Norm in person, because if I did it any other way, he was going to think I was in on it. It didn't help much because to this day he still thinks that I was. I get it; I was the bookie's liaison and the guy who introduced them to each other. It wasn't a good day. Norm was furious. He blamed me, he accused me of stealing from him, and I've never seen him so upset. To tell you the truth, it was some scary shit. I don't think anyone has ever seen Norm so upset. Eventually he calmed down, and I was able to convince him I'd never steal from him and that our friendship was worth way more than $100,000 to me. After all, that's not very much. If you add another zero to that number, it's a different story.

12

THE SPORTS HALL OF SHAME

I've made and lost a lot of money betting on sports, much more than cards, horses, or everything else degenerate gamblers bet on—which is everything, by the way. I played sports and followed sports as a kid, I talked about sports with all my friends, and from the time I was fifteen on, I bet on sports. It was a natural fit for me. I still gamble, but not nearly as much as I used to, which has taught me that I don't know as much about sports as I thought I did. Let me tell you, there is no one that knows more about professional sports than the guy who bets with a bookie every week. He knows stats, he knows who might be traded, he knows college prospects, he knows who has the best draft picks. And he knows this for every sport, every season, with no days off. If you have a friend like that or meet a guy in a bar that fits the bill, test my theory. Name a stat, he'll know it. Ask him who won the NCAA finals six years ago and what the score was, he'll know it. His girlfriend, if he has one, probably thinks that sports are just his thing the way reality TV is her thing, but his male friends know the truth: he's a degenerate gambler. Once I stopped gambling weekly, I also realized that I'm not that huge of a Giants fan. To be honest, I've completely stopped caring about how average they happen to be each season. There is one thing I have retained from my heavy betting days, however, and that is an intimate knowledge of who and where to find the ugliest people in sports and sports betting. Why is that, you ask? Because it takes one to know one.

THE 1986 BOSTON CELTICS

When I was nineteen, the 1986 Boston Celtics cost me $16,250, which is a lot when you're only making $12,000 a year. At the time, I was working union construction jobs and was at the bottom of the totem pole in my district, so I wasn't getting called in much. I was already a degenerate gambler, betting a thousand bucks when I had five hundred and washing it all down with beer, weed, and cheap coke. I've made and lost a lot more than $16,250 in a year, or even on one bet, since then, but in terms of my earnings-to-losses percentage, I'd say that my nineteenth was my most degenerate year. I had to borrow money to cover my losses, which set me on a path that never really got better until show business bailed me out.

And for this, I blame the 1986 Celtics. Now what I'm about to say might sound like nothing but bitterness and anger, but I assure you, it's not. It's been a while, and I've thought about it and I still feel confident when I say that the 1986 Boston Celtics are the ugliest championship team in the history of sports. I'm not just talking about basketball

Dennis Johnson's terrified game face. *(Kevin Reece/Icon Sportswire)*

Johnson realizing that he left the wood chipper on. *(Cliff Welch/Icon Sportswire)*

either; this claim goes all the way back to the time of the Athenians. This is no blind shot from the free throw line; I'm being completely serious. And I'm going to defend my argument with photos and a brief analysis of each player on the team's starting line to prove my point.

Dennis Johnson, point guard: a black man with reddish hair and freckles. That would be enough, but when he played he had a horrified pout for a game face. The pout was mixed with terror and surprise, as if he'd constantly just learned that his cat had been run over by a car or that his mother had fallen into a wood chipper. The pout was accented by big dark circles under his eyes and moles within those circles. He was the direct opposite of cool on every level. It didn't help that he played in an era where short shorts and knee-high white socks were the norm. Sitting here reviewing the tape, I've concluded that Dennis

Note Kevin McHale's nearly basketball-sized skull. *(Kevin Reece/Icon Sportswire)*

McHale swatting his opponent like Rodan in Japan. *(Kevin Reece/Icon Sportswire)*

Johnson made two distinct facial expressions while on the court, both of which are pictured. The first expression is how he would look watching a bear eat his mother, and the second is how he would look a few hours later, watching his mother being shit out by the bear.

Kevin McHale, power forward: Built like Frankenstein, he had sharp, pointed bones on each shoulder that made him look like an experiment. On top of his dome sat short, dark black hair that looked like it had been cut by a blind barber from 1932. McHale possessed an odd, misshaped, abnormally large cranium. His skull was frightening to children and disproportionate to everything else on his entire body. Rushing down the court, he looked like Rodan, coming to wreak havoc on a small Japanese village.

Robert Parish, center: Parish always looked like someone had just asked him the hardest question on the SAT. His nickname was "the Chief," because his teammates said he was as stoic as the character in *One Flew Over the Cuckoo's Nest,* but really it was because he looked like a cigar-store Indian statue. His forehead had an extra piece of meat that came down over his eyes, which made him look angry no

Angry as ever, Robert Parish dunking. *(Kevin Reece/Icon Sportswire)*

matter how he felt. If you put a party hat on him and a New Year's Eve noisemaker in his mouth and asked him to smile, it wouldn't change a thing. If he tried to act happy,

Bill Walton using hideousness to outwit the opposition. *(John Mc Donough/Icon Sportswire)*

Walton: Phil Lesh meets the Joker. *(John Mc Donough/Icon Sportswire)*

he'd end up looking like Hitler giving a speech at the 1934 Nuremberg rally. That was the best you could do hoping to capture a joyous Robert Parish in 1986. To be fair, it's not really his fault, because that extra skin forces his eyes to slant down, making him look forever full of rage. Between Dennis Johnson's pout and Robert Parish's glare, it doesn't get any worse. If you took a photo of them facing each other, it would look like Parish was about to make Johnson cry.

Bill Walton, center: He was everything I just said about Robert Parish, but white. He is also a Deadhead, so he wore tie-dyed shirts in public, which exaggerated his insane ugliness. He looked like what would happen if Phil Lesh were dropped in acid and survived, like the Joker. By the time Walton got to the Celtics, he was thirty-three, which is sixty years old in basketball years. He was over the hill, wrinkled, stuttered, and spoke with a crazy lisp.

At one point, Larry Bird was almost cool.
(John Mc Donough/Icon Sportswire)

Larry Bird: Where the Muppets meet *Sesame Street*. (*Zuma Press*/Icon Sportswire)

Fire up the shish kebob, Boston, it's almost Larry Bird Day! *(Darrell Walker/Icon Sportswire)*

That is a lot of ugly in one package. A guy from Boston once told me that Bill Walton looked like a guy who actually went to college. I wasn't sure what he meant, so I asked him. "Because he's white," he said.

Larry Bird, small forward: Let me begin by saying that I want to think of Larry Bird as good-looking. I really do. He's one of the greatest to ever play the game, and in 1982, when he was younger, there was a moment when, if you gave him a quick glance, for one second, he might have been good-looking. He had blond shaggy hair and a mustache. Mustaches were cool, and he could have been cool, but he ruined his chances the moment he cut his hair into that awful mullet. It is universal karma that his last name is Bird. Born with a huge, pointy nose that hooks completely down and a big chin that juts out farther than it should, he looks like nothing else on earth but a large, awkward bird. To me, he's a combination of the eagle from the Muppets and Big Bird from *Sesame Street*. Over the years, his pointy nose and massive chin have grown closer and closer together, which I've found very unsettling. If I held a legislative position in the city of Boston, I would anticipate the day that his nose and chin meet and declare it a holiday. This is sure to happen in the next three to five years. When the Holland Tunnel was being built in the 1920s, one crew of workers started in New York and another started in New Jersey. My grandfather liked telling me the story of how, when the two sides met, they had a party, and New York City had a big celebration. To me, Boston should be just as proud of the progress Larry Bird's nose and chin are making on their journey to become one. When they finally connect, the city of Boston should take at least a week or two off and celebrate with free shish kebabs for everyone, because that will be the only food Larry will be able to shove into his mouth through the side. They should also rename the MBTA's downtown bus loop "Larry Bird Loop" in his honor. It will be like Boston's Bastille Day with a film adaptation starring Mark Wahlberg.

K. C. Jones leading his team in looking good.
(John McDonough/Icon Sportswire)

I'd like to point out that none of this is as terrifying as Dennis Johnson, a red-haired African American with freckles.

K. C. Jones, coach: His name

explains Bill Walton's dedication to the team. In Bill's mind, Coach was driving that train, high on cocaine. K. C. was a former player who turned into a chubby, conservative-looking guy after retirement. Looking at the picture on page 154, he resembles none other than Tracy Morgan after his car accident. I love Tracy, and I don't feel bad about making that joke, because, God bless him, Tracy is living like a lottery winner. I recently saw a picture of him in the paper standing outside of the $14 million house he'd just bought. I'm guessing that he got about $100 million in settlement money based on the fact that Ardie Fuqua, who was in the accident as well, was still broke before that Walmart money rolled in. Tracy had money, but Ardie was still living in the ghetto at forty-eight years old. Now he's got a fire-engine-red Cadillac Escalade, a huge Range Rover, and wears a different Brooks Brothers blazer onstage every night. He was on a bill with me recently, so I did this joke: "I hear Tracy Morgan pays $25 million to open for him." It killed.

Danny Ainge, guard: I know what a lot of you guys are saying. Maybe you're Celtics fans or maybe not, but I hear you saying, "Art, you're wrong. Not all the '86 Celtics were ugly. Danny Ainge was good-looking." My answer to you is, "Stop reading this immediately, return to the store, and exchange it for Aziz Ansari's book, you fruit."

Danny Aigne rubbing up on Magic Johnson.
(Zuma Press/Icon Sportswire)

(left to right) Ken Griffey Sr., the odd-looking Joe Morgan, and Pete Rose. *(Ken Stewart/Zuma Press/Icon Sportswire)*

Dave Concepcion's million-dollar smile. *(Owen C. Shaw/Icon Sportsswire)*

Pete Rose's modeling head shot, 1975. *(Ken Stewart/Zuma Press/Icon Sportswire)*

AS FAR AS MY LARGER argument regarding the supreme ugliness of the 1986 Boston Celtics, you can say, "Art, you're right." If you are sensible and logical, that's what you'll do; you'll say, "Art, you're right." The more cynical among you may feel that I'm miscalculating, and some of you may even claim that there are uglier teams—for example, the 1975 Cincinnati Reds featuring such male models as Pete Rose, Joe Morgan—who was a *very* odd-looking guy—and Dave Concepcion. You are welcome to your opinion, but I don't agree with you at all.

On a side note, I once had sex with a stripper that looked like Pete Rose. I met her at a club called Lace in Nyack,

New York, after a gig at a nearby comedy club. We really hit it off, so she came to see me do a set at Caroline's in the city, and afterward I talked her back to my place in Hoboken. This was when my ex-fiancée, Adrienne, and I were on a break because we'd been fighting so much that she moved out. Anyway, this stripper was Russian and knew nothing about Pete Rose or baseball, so I was able to call her his nickname, Charlie Hustle, without her knowing what I was talking about. "Charlie Hustle, get in here!" She thought it was a cute nickname I'd made up just for her. She and I broke my bed, by the way. She was very athletic sexually, she really knew how to slide into home, but it wasn't her fault. I'm fat, so the thing just fell to the floor while I was humping her. For the record, during sex, I got her to admit that she'd gambled on baseball while employed as a manager.

The lesson here is that the 1986 Boston Celtics cost me, at the age of nineteen, $16,250. As I mentioned, I was into drinking and drugs, and mixing those with gambling is a lot of fun, but it typically has disastrous side effects. Here's an example. The under-over in a Boston-NY basketball game was usually about 190 points back then. The odds in baseball are usually minus 200. One time that year, my bookie, Bobo, took advantage of how drunk I was when I called him. He let me place my bet on a baseball game as if it were a basketball game. Making bets in a blackout is never a good idea.

The next day, I asked him, "Why would you think that? No baseball game in history has ever had 190 runs."

"I did it because you need to be taught a lesson," he said.

"Thanks, Mr. Bookie," I said. "Have I just earned my degree from gambling university?"

OTB

OTB, which was opened in 1971 in an effort to funnel the profits that bookies made on horse racing back into the city, closed in 2010, so you'll have to take my word for it when I tell you what those places were like. There were fifty of them in Manhattan and the outer boroughs, and I used to frequent the one on Seventh Avenue and Thirty-eighth Street when I was driving a cab. Usually I'd stop in during off hours, in the middle of the day. It was the type of place every student of anthropology should have seen because it was chock-full of humans that you didn't see anywhere else. It was like a Starbucks for insanely degenerate gamblers who were too lazy to go to racetracks like Aqueduct or Belmont, where, by the way, they have lunch specials several days a week. Not even the promise of two-dollar plates of chicken could tempt these specimens to leave their dingy, off-track cave. Those lunches, which I have seen with my own eyes, were also worthy of study by scientists, because, for two dollars, you could get chicken sitting under fluorescent lights so harsh that you were able to see the veins and the connective tissue, and if you looked closely, you could trace the entire life cycle of the chicken. It was like those chickens were starring in the Albert Brooks film *Defending Your Life* in which the main character stands trial in the afterlife, justifying his fears and decisions in order to progress to the great beyond. Looking down on those once-living things, I could see it all: the chicken born, tortured, killed, cooked, and left to be examined by losers like me.

Anyway, the daytime crowds at OTB were fascinating. I have no idea how they became who they were, because it clearly didn't happen overnight. If I were forced to re-create one in a lab, here is what I'd do. I'd go to a White Castle in East Orange, New Jersey, at 4:00 a.m. and find, as Jimmy the Greek would say, "the biggest buck." Then I'd go to the grimiest DMV in the city and look for the crowd of people who go there just to hang out and talk. Believe me, those people exist, because I've met them. Next time you're forced to go to into one of those hellholes of bureaucracy, look around and you'll see them in the waiting area, waiting to talk to you. They don't have a number and aren't concerned about the line, and they usually have a Big Gulp, a lot of questions, and elastic-waist pants. Anyway, I'd go to a dirty DMV and find the biggest woman in that group and mate her with the biggest buck I'd poached from White Castle. Then, I'd wait until their offspring was of age and mate it with the entire upper deck at a Philadelphia Eagles home game. I'd wait again, and when that child was born, I'd take it and raise it in a barn and never teach it hygiene. After about twenty-four years, I'd do the humane thing and set it free in an OTB during the day, where it would feel right at home. Another way to replicate an OTB regular would be to go to a Phish concert—where, by the way, Bill Walton would fit right in—and find a kid who has been doing nothing but following them for about fifteen years. He would need to be about 38 years old and to have spent the better part of his life shitting in port-o-johns. I say "he" because women were there, but they were few and far between at OTB. Now as filthy, shifty, and disgusting as these people were, they had something in common: they were all good at handicapping races. They analyzed horse stats 'round the clock and were great at assessing the lineup and the handicaps and wagering their cash to make a few bucks. For most of them, it looked to be their full-time job.

Back then, a kid I knew who worked in my hometown bar and did some side work with a connected bookie used to give me tips, sometimes on college games and sometimes on horses. When he did, I'd go to OTB to place my bet, and since I'm a people person, I'd ask a regular what he thought of the horse. Usually the guy wouldn't even look up from his racing paper.

"So what do you think of Daffy Darling in the sixth?" I'd ask.

"Piece of shit. Only there to round out the field."

"Thanks. I appreciate that."

And then Daffy Darling would win, because if the kid had given me a tip on a horse, it was definitely a fix. Horse races are the easiest events to fix, and usually it happens a few ways. Crooked trainers and owners will give the horse a shot of something illegal to increase its stamina or, when they see a light field, one way or another, they'll make sure that the other horses aren't able to do their best. It's not hard to regulate since there are only five horses in most races, so that's not a lot of competition to sabotage. They will literally stab another horse so that it can't perform at its peak or stash its head in the bed of a movie producer who crossed the family.

OLE MISS VERSUS AIR FORCE

The kid who gave me tips was right 100 percent of the time when it came to horses. When it came to sports, not so much. In 1992, Ole Miss and Air Force were in the Liberty Bowl, and the line was nine. The kid told me that he had inside information that Ole Miss was only going to score thirteen points. That was a weird, very specific number, so I believed him. What that means is that if Ole Miss, the favorite to win, was given nine points and only scored thirteen, they probably would not cover that nine-point spread. Even if Air Force sucked and had the worst day in the history of the team, all they had to do was score one touchdown for me to cover my point spread and win some money. This was a no-brainer bet. I can't remember how much I put down, but it was a lot, because this guy had given me foolproof tips at the track, so I trusted him. In the end, Ole Miss won 13–0. All I needed was one touchdown, and I didn't get it, so I was pissed.

"What the fuck, man?" I asked him. "That tip was shit."

"Hey, don't blame me," he said. "They did what I told you they would do. They scored thirteen points."

Clearly, my degree from Gambling U wasn't worth shit.

SUPER BOWL XXXVIII: CAROLINA PANTHERS VERSUS NEW ENGLAND PATRIOTS

This one has been discussed in the other books, but I bring it up again because I have details to add that make it a worthy entry into the Sports Hall of Shame. First of all, it's a famous Super Bowl because the over didn't look good and also because Janet Jackson's pierced nipple fell out on national television. Both teams went scoreless in the first and third quarters, and by halftime the combined score was twenty-four points. Then Tom Brady did his thing in the fourth quarter, because he can beat anyone in the second half with the exception of Eli Manning, which I find so odd. That is why I insist that there's something off about Tom Brady: he's blessed against every quarterback in the league except a mouth breather who looks like a mongoloid. That guy is his kryptonite? Really? Lucky for him, the Giants usually beat themselves most of the time.

Anyway, that weekend, I was booked to do two shows at the Mirage in Vegas, at $60,000 per show, plus they gave me another $20,000 to host an after party at their stupid club, Jet. I was looking at a $140,000 weekend. It was going to be great. I was still dating Dana, who called me with an urgent message: she and her mother wanted to place bets on the Super Bowl. They wanted to bet the over-under. This was a first.

"So how much do you want to bet?" I asked.

"Okay, I've thought about it, and I want fifty dollars on the over, and so does Mom."

"Okay, I got it."

I hung up, having no intention of placing that bet because I would never bet fifty dollars on anything. That's even less than "just the tip" in my book. Then I realized that Dana was all excited about this and was the type of person who would want to see the casino ticket from the sports betting room at the casino as if it were an invitation to a bachelorette party. So I went down to the sports booker in the hotel, placed their bets for fifty dollars each, got the tickets, and called her back.

"Okay, I did it. You're both in for fifty."

She was thrilled and very enthusiastic. "Oh, this is so fun! Well, let's root for you too; what do you have in?"

"I have $20,000 on the under," I said. "Good luck."

The game will go down in history as one of the most well-played and thrilling games in Super Bowl history. The over won, of course, so I lost my $20,000. The only upside was that someone at a Jet game got me a whore who I fucked with my socks on. She blew me in the bathroom and was so sexy that I asked the guy if she could come back to my room. He made that happen, so when I was allowed to leave, she came with me and I fucked her, and never have I felt like more of a loser while fucking one of the sexiest girls I've ever seen. She redefined the word *stoic*. Have you seen the Clint Eastwood film *Sudden Impact*? Sondra Locke's character gets gang-raped, and she sits there, catatonic as it's happening, and this girl's expression was a dead ringer. Actually, that combined with the look on the dead horse's face in *The Godfather*.

"I must have been really good," I said to her afterward.

"Why do you say that?"

"Because you put the magazine down for a minute."

The only time I saw emotion flicker across her face was when I went to get her some money. At first she stopped me.

"You don't need to pay me; I'm taken care of," she said.

"Let me just get you some money. I insist."

As I walked over to the safe, she covered her mouth and started giggling.

"What? What's so funny?"

"Your socks," she said, barely getting the words out. "You kept your socks on."

She was young and already soulless, God bless her. She had not one shred of innocence or humanity left. Then she sold me some Ecstasy and left.

It was quite the weekend, which, by anyone's standards, would look to be a winner. Anyone but me, that is. I took in $140,000, but after gambling, whores, drugs, food, strippers who didn't tell me they were whores until we were in my room, more whores, and Dana and her mother's winnings (which I forgot to pick up and had to pay out of my own money), I ended up down $5,000. Dana was so excited to have won her bet that she asked for it right away, and you can't imagine how hard it was for me to fork that over. I would have rather given her teeth from my own head, pulled out with a pair of pliers. The only thing worse than adding up my losses on the plane home was walking into my accountant's office. He was sitting there behind his desk expecting a check for $140,000.

"Great game, wasn't it, Art? And you really cleaned up out there. I'm going to take the taxes out now and—"

"Yeah, about that," I said. "Change of plan. I need a check for $5,000."

13

NOW EVERYTHING'S HAPPENED

Everyone loves stories of winning big at the tables, of the impossible craps run, of hitting ten-to-one odds on a game or a horse. It's the Lotto, it's the American dream, it's the golden ticket and the oasis we all want to believe exists in this desert we call life. It's the snake oil that keeps people going, because human beings need to believe in something. The thing most people don't talk about when it comes to gambling is the losing. Unless you're addicted to thrills and allergic to boredom like I am, losing is the embarrassment you sweep under the rug.

Organized gambling, legal and otherwise, is a losing proposition for the gambler, so unless you accept that, you're kidding yourself. I embrace it and I enjoy it, because I get the same jolt of adrenaline when I lose as I do when I win. That's because when I lose, I lose big. My losses are like a huge ship passing by, trailing a wake of chaos, and there I am, having the time of my life, just an asshole on a

Jet Ski catching air off the backwash. I will forever be bitter about certain losses and certain teams and players who have cost me tens of thousands of dollars over the years, but I don't begrudge the excitement. Since I'm lucky enough that I've been able to keep earning money, I don't think I'd trade the memories for my cash back.

Naturally, when it comes to betting with my life, I apply the same philosophy. Unfortunately for me, the game I lose biggest at is the one I can't stop playing, and that game is a roulette called drugs. I just can't stay away from them, and it's not cool or something I'm proud of. I'm an addict, and I do my best to stay sober and keep from letting opiates and cocaine destroy all the good things I have going for me, but it ain't easy, man. Drugs are a surefire way to dial up the unknown. Because, much like the way I bet, when I do drugs, I go big.

About a year ago, I fell off the wagon after a year of being completely clean. I went on a two-week bender that couldn't have come at a worse time. I was arrested because the cops caught me with a lot of heroin and cocaine, and because of that, I ended up under indictment. I went to court over that incident and put it behind me, but then, in early 2017, I fucked up again and got arrested for possession once more, this time sitting in my car, in the basement garage of my condo. Luckily, Hoboken is an old-school kind of town, so I was able to make some calls and pull in some favors and managed to get my charges reduced so that I didn't do hard time.

Anyway, let's go back to that first slipup, because drug stories and gambling stories are both studies in risk, which is what I'm trying to make sense of here. Remember a few chapters back when I admitted to cheating on Dana with Vegas strippers eleven times in a week? Well, there's more to that, because it wasn't a onetime thing. It wasn't a case of "what happens in Vegas stays in Vegas"—it was a case of "what happens every time I leave town stays in whatever town I go to."

Vegas was extraordinary in terms of the quality of the women available to me, but when I was on *Stern* and doing stand-up on the weekends, there was a chick waiting for me in every city because it was just *so fucking easy*. I could never talk about it on the air, because I was with Dana, but now, fuck it, I don't care what she knows or thinks of me anymore. She has a baby, and we live very different lives. She contacted me recently, and I was happy about it, because we shared a lot and she really knows me. I'd hoped that I could have her in my life again as a close friend in some way, but that's impossible. The last time we spoke, we got into the kind of nasty argument that made me realize that as sad as it is, we can never be friends. Which means that I don't care about protecting her memories of us anymore.

So I had a chick in every city, and things could not have been better. They would literally be waiting for me at my gigs or in the hotel lobby in every single town I visited. They'd meet up with me, we'd hang out, and no one was the wiser. I'm talking beautiful chicks who just wanted to get on the *Stern Show*. It was easier than shooting fish in a barrel! You might find this hard to believe, but I'm no ladies' man. Until my gig at *Stern*, it was a tremendous effort for me to get laid, but bagging broads on the road was so easy that even my friend Mike Bocchetti could have done it.

I was always staying at a nice hotel taken care of by the promoter, so I'd pay for a room next to mine where I'd send a girl to hang out and wait for me until my show was over. Then we'd fuck and I'd keep her number, and every time I flew into Boston or Cleveland or wherever, I'd call her and we'd do it all again. I'd tell her the hotel and the room number I'd reserved under her name and that was that. It was as easy as ordering room service.

These chicks were the pick of the litter too. There was one in Tempe, Arizona, that I will never forget until the day I die. She looked like a young Nicole Eggert with long blond hair, a flat stomach, and perfect tits. I get great crowds in Tempe too, so she'd see me kill in a sold-out theater that held about three thousand, which made it all the better, because to a comedy groupie, that's an aphrodisiac. It gets them wet. It's the equivalent of a band groupie watching the show before blowing the guitar player. We had a great relationship, Young Eggert and I: she'd enjoy my set, then back at the hotel she'd tell me about her hard-knock life, I'd say, "Sure, I will buy your mother a new motor home," and we'd have sex all night.

Anyway, I went on that two-week drug rampage with a chick I'd met in Boston back in the *Stern* days. That's where she was from, and that's where I bumped into her again. In 2002, she was a twenty-three-year-old 10. In December 2015, she was a thirty-six-year-old 8. She'd had two kids but was still smoking hot and was even more troubled than she used to be. She also had a thick Southie accent, which is hilarious on a hot chick. A sexy girl can be dressed to the nines in a gown fit for the Oscars, but if she speaks Southie, no matter what she says, she sounds like she's heckling a Yankee batter from the bleachers in Fenway.

When I walked into the lobby of the hotel that winter, there she was. I hadn't talked to her in years and had no intention of doing so. Things were going well for me: my podcast was gaining listeners steadily month to month, my calendar was filled with stand-up gigs, Anthony and I were working on the third book, I was in talks with two different networks about my next one-hour comedy special, and I'd been cast on Judd Apatow's new project, *Crashing*, which began shooting in three weeks. There was no logical reason to risk any of that. But she was a hot chick with blow, and my life had been stable for too long.

For the next two weeks, we were joined at the hip. I brought her on the road with me, and we had a grand old time fucking, ordering room service, and doing drugs. Our little traveling narcotics orgy culminated with me getting arrested in Jersey, after things came apart in Pittsburgh when I got a nosebleed onstage. It was December on the East Coast, when pollen counts are nonexistent, but I insisted to everyone I knew that I was suffering from allergies so bad that I'd cut the inside of my nose from blowing it too hard. I was blowing it, all right.

Here's what really happened. I was at the Four Seasons in New York with the Sexy Southie, which is where I put her up when I was back home between gigs, because I didn't want her at my apartment. We were there, we were partying, and I went to take a shower. I told her to order us some room service, which she did, and when it came, she decided to chop up some OxyContin right there on the tray. She did the smart thing and used a saltshaker to crush the pill, smashing the lower glass part to bits. She picked out the big pieces and tried to rescue the drugs but still ended up with a pile of salt, glass shards, and Oxy. She didn't snort any of it, because who would do that? But since she was high, she forgot to mention this blunder to me when I got out of the shower.

If you're not into opiates, you've got to trust me when I say that after a nice hot shower, when you're wearing a fancy terry cloth bathrobe in a five-star hotel, nothing could be better than a line of Oxy. When the Sexy Southie went into the bathroom to shower, I sat down, looked at the pile of drugs, and thought, *Wasn't that nice of her to set me up like that.*

After two weeks of abuse, my tolerance was high, so I cut a generous line and snorted it up my right nostril. When the mixture of salt, glass, and Oxy tore into my mucus membranes, the white-hot pain was what I think it must be like to have a hot poker shoved somewhere it shouldn't be, like your ear or your ass. Despite the drugs in my system, it was so arresting that time stood still long enough for me to calmly think, *Something is very wrong here*, before my vision blurred and I started screaming. It felt as if my nose was held together by a zipper that someone had just violently unzipped.

Well, now everything's happened, I thought. It was something I'd been thinking nearly every day for the past two weeks as the bender continued to escalate. Each time things got worse and more insane, I kept thinking, *Well, now everything's happened*. And then something worse would happen, so I'd think, *No, that wasn't it before. This is it.* Now *everything's happened*. I had the right to make that distinction, because I'd just snorted a line of glass and salt, which was something that had not happened before. I was even more pissed off when I remembered that we were in the Four Seasons. That saltshaker probably cost me eighty-two dollars.

I'm not judging, but the Sexy Southie wasn't exactly Stephen Hawking. Do I need to point this out? Who grabs a glass saltshaker to break up a pill? There were plates, silverware, bottles of booze, hotel card keys, her phone—so many sturdier options. It was the Four Seasons! She could have called the concierge and had someone come up to crush the pill for her! I'm sure it wouldn't have been the first time.

I ran into the bathroom, yelling at the top of my lungs, half-blind with pain.

"Artie! What's the matta? Ya' bleedin!'" she said.

"Oh, you don't say!" I screamed. "I know I'm fucking bleeding! What the hell was that?"

"Oh, Artie, I'm sorry, I broke the shaka crushing up the pill. I meant to tell ya."

"Goddammit! My nose is now high in sodium, thank you very much! Don't you know that I have high blood pressure?"

This happened precisely one week before my first day on set with Judd Apatow. I'd gambled, I'd lost, and I was fucked. I didn't have time to have a top surgeon clear the glass out of my nose. I had two gigs that week, one of them the next night.

I washed out the blood and glass as best I could and did drugs up the other nostril to kill the pain. That worked a bit, but my nose was such a mess that I had to take Oxy the old-fashioned way, which is a lot less fun. My nose swelled up immediately, and I looked like I'd been in a fight, because, over the next few days, I developed a shiner under my right eye. By the time I got to Pittsburgh the next night, I still looked okay, by which I mean my usual level of disheveled, which hovers just above homeless. My entire forehead sinus area on the right side felt like it had been smashed with a hammer, but I was highly medicated, so I managed to keep it together and get onstage. Everything was fine until my nose started bleeding profusely in front of a sold-out club full of a thousand people. Whatever nerve endings I had left in my nose had been shredded by that glass line, so I didn't even feel it until the blood started dripping so thickly that it ran down my shirt and onto my hands.

I wiped my face on my sleeve, which made things worse, tried to ignore it all, and continued my act.

"Artie, your nose is bleeding," said a voice to my right. A kid who worked for the club had come onstage with a towel. That's how bad it was. "Here, Artie, take this."

When a guy comes onstage in front of a thousand people to give you a towel because you're unaware that your nose is bleeding so heavily that it's grossing out the audience, I'd say it's time to take a look in the mirror.

"Oh, is it?" I asked. "Thanks, man. Allergies." I watched the towel turn red as I tried to stop the flow. Then I turned to the audience and said, "Well, guys, now everything's happened."

At least that's what I thought, but no, everything hadn't happened yet.

The nosebleed was my cue that the jig was up, however.

I'd hit a wall with this little party, and I was done. I knew what I had to do: get rid of the Sexy Southie, start weaning myself off the opiates, and get back to normal. I finished my set, went directly to an AA meeting, and started pumping the brakes on my latest slide into the abyss.

My nose would not stop bleeding, however, so after the meeting I went to the emergency room, where some intern did a hatchet job on whatever was left of the cartilage in my septum. I told the girl from Boston that if I ever saw her again I'd take out a restraining order against her and said that none of this was her fault but that I was weak and couldn't be anywhere near her. I reminded her that she had two kids to take care of at home and told her not to ask me for money or anything ever again. "It's not just the blow and the opiates," I said. "It's you and me. I can't keep doing any of this." And so we said goodbye.

One week later I was on set with the greatest comedy producer of this generation. After the invasive surgery, I looked like Gerry Cooney after thirteen rounds with Larry Holmes: lopsided and swollen with a black eye. The makeup girls worked miracles, but they couldn't keep my nose from bleeding during every take for the first two days of shooting. Let's just say that no one bought my allergies excuse. Quite a return to scripted television!

I had to be constantly cleaned up and blotted, but all things considered, I killed in my scenes and Judd was happy with my performance. I don't think there is a more understanding, collaborative, and inventive film and television creator working today. Instead of seeing a negative, Judd turned it into a positive and wrote a nosebleed into the show. It ultimately didn't make the final cut, but we shot some scenes where we let my nose bleed and made it into a running joke, no pun intended.

I saw a better doctor while we were shooting, and he operated on me but told me from the start that the damage had been done. The first guy had hacked out a lot of cartilage and left behind a lot of scar tissue. My nose will never be the same; it is forever unzipped. To get all the glass out, the doctor basically removed whatever was left of my septum after thirty years of doing drugs. Put it this way: if I sneeze while I'm eating cake, I sneeze cake. Yesterday I laughed at lunch and half a sub sandwich flew out one side of my nose.

So my nose bled on and off throughout the shoot, and I was mortified. I tried my best to be as funny as possible to make up for it, and Judd could not have been cooler. We were shooting a major-budget HBO comedy series, and he didn't even care. He was more concerned that I get help and get better. And for him, for me, and for everyone I was working with on the show, I wanted to.

But everything hadn't happened yet.

After the shoot wrapped, I was still weaning myself off the opiates. I knew how to do it, because it wasn't my first time, so I went out and bought as much as I'd need to slowly dial things down. Then I got arrested with that stash in New Jersey, driving home, just a few miles from my house. I was cuffed and stuffed, my car was impounded, and I spent a cold February night in jail. I have a lot of fans in law enforcement, especially in North Jersey, but that didn't help me this time. I was busted and booked by a woman cop who was clearly campaigning for rookie of the year. She made Sergeant Joe Friday look like Detective Frank Drebin.

When we got to the precinct and she saw that every other cop there was a fan, it inspired her to be even more of a hard-ass. It really ruffled her feathers when one guy went to his cruiser and came back with a copy of *Too Fat to Fish*. He told me that he'd kept it in the car for over a year, hoping to see me driving around town so he could pull me over and get it signed. That night he got his wish.

The only upside of that female officer being by the book is that she forbade anyone from calling the press. Still, I need to take a moment to thank whoever at TMZ put a kibosh on publicizing that arrest. I will be forever grateful, and I owe them a major favor. When I was busted for a DUI a few years back, someone called them, and a guy with a camera showed up in fifteen minutes. It was out to the world before I even got home, and I was less than a mile from my beach house.

I'm glad they gave me a pass this time, because I was busted with a lot of drugs. It didn't look good, but to tell you the truth, I knew what I was doing: I made sure I wouldn't have to go out and get more. I planned for one trip to the dealer and bought enough to have a little bit more fun and then taper off and be done with it again. But life threw me a curveball, I got arrested, and in the end I was so mad at myself for fucking things up that when I got out of jail I didn't bother getting anything to ease the withdrawals. I did them cold turkey. That's never a good time, but if you've read my second book, *Crash and Burn*, you know that I've been through worse.

Before that, though, I spent the night in a jail cell with a very heavyset African American gentleman who was straight out of central casting. He was Hispanic, actually;

as I recall, he said he was three-quarters Puerto Rican, one-quarter black. He had straight hair, or as Chris Rock would say, "good hair," and weighed about 350 pounds. This was a county jail, so the cell was small, and we had bunk beds, and by law I had to stay there until 9:00 the next morning.

I'd made my one phone call—to my producer and lifeline, Dan Falato—to tell him what had happened and when to pick me up. To tell you the truth, I was relieved, because the three-week whirlwind was over. I was exhausted and coming down, so even in such tight quarters, I looked forward to getting some sleep. I tried to put the repercussions of the arrest out of my mind. Most likely I'd be fired from *Crashing*. Hell, they still had time to recut things and eliminate my character from the show altogether. That didn't happen, but it was all I could think of sitting there that night. I don't know what it's all about; I guess I just have *dat ting*. I feel like someone is watching over me, because somehow I ended up tiptoeing through the raindrops again.

Around 4:00 a.m., I woke up, not uncomfortable but aware of something not being where it should be. The only way to describe it is that there was a presence and it was close to me. I was lying on my back on the lower bunk, and as I slowly regained consciousness, I realized that something warm and large was lying against my head. It was clammy, too, just a bit too moist.

If you haven't had the pleasure of spending a night in a county jail cell, here's what it's like. They're fucking small, for one thing, with enough room for a bunk bed, a tiny sink, a toilet and nothing else. At most, the toilet is two

feet from the bed, which means that you and your cellmate shit in front of each other because there's no place to
hide.

When I opened my eyes, I realized that my cellmate was
shitting. Actually, that's not quite right; he wasn't shitting
at that moment, but he had been shitting. He was still sitting on the toilet, pants down, but was now sleeping. His
body had relaxed so his naked leg had drifted and was flat
against my head. He was also snoring and had been asleep
some time, because a layer of sweat had glued his leg to my
forehead.

"Hey, man, what the fuck?" I said.

Before I could pull my head away, he grumbled, groaned,
kind of farted, and then *plop*, took another shit. It was a
knee-jerk reaction, like I'd startled him and literally scared
that shit out of him. The worst part about it was that his
knee was still against my head, so I felt it happen. It vibrated
my face because it wasn't a smooth exit; it sounded like a
chain saw cutting through a log. It was the most awkward
and oddly intimate moment I've ever shared with another
human being.

"Dude," I said, "your knee is on my head."

He turned, looked at me, and said, "Oh, my bad."

Then he peeled his knee from my forehead, and it made
a squelchy noise.

Thank God the guy had a sense of humor, because I
couldn't contain myself.

"'My bad,'" I said. "Really? 'My bad'? Are you kidding
me? 'My bad' is what you say when your kid's whiffle ball
accidentally hits my car. When your knee is resting on me
in a jail cell while you shit and I feel the release through

my face, it ain't 'My bad!' It's 'Oh my God! We need immediate counseling!'"

"You right, man," he said, chuckling. "That was fucked up."

"We should wake up the desk sergeant and tell him what
happened. At least he'll get a good fucking laugh. It ain't
'my bad,' dude."

"No, man, you right; it ain't 'my bad.'"

As I rolled over to go back to sleep, I knew one thing for
sure. This event reset the bar. As exhaustion washed over
me and I began to drift off, I found solace in just one thing.
Well, that was it, I thought. *No doubt about it*. Now *everything's
happened*.

14

HOLLYWOOD WIGS, VALLEY HEAD

In 1997, I was in Canada with Norm Macdonald shooting *Dirty Work*, and Adam Sandler came on set for one day to do his cameo as Satan. One of our producers on the film was Robert Simonds, who is a famous and very successful Hollywood figure. He's also Lorne Michaels's archnemesis because he's taken many *SNL* cast members that Lorne hadn't scooped up for film projects and made them into movie stars, most notably Steve Martin and Adam Sandler. By then, he'd gotten Sandler well on his way with *Airheads*, *Happy Gilmore*, *Billy Madison*, and the film they'd just wrapped, *The Wedding Singer*.

That movie would push Adam into the stratosphere, but that day on set with us, just back from shooting in Hawaii, he was so frustrated with it.

"Guys, whatever you do, never do a movie with a wig," he said.

"Really?"

"Oh my God, man. Worst thing you could ever do. It's like having a stuffed animal on your head every day. It's hot, it's itchy, and underneath it your hair is plastered down with glue."

The next movie I did was *Lost and Found*, playing David Spade's loser sidekick, and when they placed the wig on my head every morning, I thought of Sandler. What he hadn't mentioned was that when you have a wig, it comes with a whole team whose job it is to look after the thing. There was the wig expert who fitted the wig before shooting and her staff of assistants who were on set every day. There were more people on the payroll to handle my wig than there would have been to handle live animals. My wig fitter was Renée of Burbank, the most famous wig lady in the business. She had about forty-two cats, had been living in the same house for probably forty-two years, and when she measured my head, she exclaimed, "Oh! You've got the same head as Chucky!"

"Chucky who?" I asked. "Chucky the doll? The doll who kills people?"

"No, I'm talking about my dear friend Charlton Heston. All of his friends call him Chucky, you know."

"Oh, okay. Does the NRA call him Chucky?"

"What was that, dear?"

"Oh, nothing. This wig feels great!"

That wig, by the way, cost $6,000 and had an insurance policy. After they put it on me in the morning, a harem of six cute girl technicians spent the day following me around, making sure it looked the same in every shot. They were there the day I accidentally dunked it into some gravy at lunch, which they handled with a smile, and they paid so much attention to me that I felt special. That lasted until the second we were done, when they'd rip the wig off my head as gently as a pit crew changing tires at a NASCAR race. Once they had the wig in their possession, they couldn't have cared less if I lived or died. But there was one woman on the makeup crew that I'll never forget, because quite frankly, she looked like me. To quote Woody Allen in *Broadway Danny Rose*, she looked "like something you'd find in a live bait shop."

She was affectionate toward me, though, even when the wig was off, because she knew how uncomfortable that thing was. Every day, after they removed it, she'd wash my hair with warm water, and she massaged my scalp so tenderly that it was a sensual experience. I'm telling you, every day, as this female ogre rinsed my hair, I almost came. It was a nice long rinse too, because it took quite a bit of glue to keep my hair matted down with the spirit gum Sandler had mentioned.

The reason my character wore a wig, by the way, and this is a joke that Spade and I both missed, was that I was supposed to be like Jennifer Jason Leigh in *Single White Female*, copying Spade's haircut since I wanted to be like him so badly. The critics saw something else altogether, because with the wig on, I looked a lot like Chris Farley, since all fat white guys look the same. Chris had just died, and critics accused Spade of trying to replace him. This point was made in most reviews of the film, none of which were favorable, and Spade couldn't believe it. He was really hurt that anyone would think that of him.

That movie *Lost and Found*—and this is saying a lot—is the worst thing I've ever done. There are funny moments, because David Spade is hilarious, but everything else was ill conceived. For example, his costar and love interest was Sophie Marceau. I saw her every morning as we got our hair and makeup done, and I realized something that until then I thought was impossible. She and I are both considered human beings, but that can't be true, because seeing us side by side, no one would take us for the same species. At 6:00 a.m., just out of bed, she was so stunningly beautiful that I couldn't help but stare. Then I'd catch a glimpse of myself and feel bad for the makeup artist who'd drawn the short straw. Now, in real life, Spade was a multimillionaire, a famous comedian, and dated beautiful women. He and Sophie were costars, and he hit on her quite a bit, but it went nowhere, because she repeatedly turned him down. In the movie, however, Spade, still looking like Spade, plays a broke guy trying to launch a restaurant, who gets her without even trying. That is why the movie bombed, in my opinion: it was billed as a comedy, but the plot was closer to science fiction. I texted this theory to Spade once and then typed *LOL* to let him know I was kidding. A moment later, he texted back, *Don't tell me when to laugh. I'm not some cheerleader you're asking to prom. I'll tell you when something's funny.*

Come to think of it, my life is basically a misconceived Hollywood film. It's not as bad as *Lost and Found;* it's a different kind of bad. It's the kind of movie that should end but keeps going. I have enjoyed many picture-perfect moments that should have been my Hollywood ending, but since this is my life, the movie continued when the credits should have rolled and instead, in the last act everything turned to shit. If my life's movie was supposed to be a romantic comedy, for example, it would end with me kissing the love of my life somewhere perfect like the Eiffel Tower, which is when it should fade to black but instead, you'd then see me throw up on her because I'm on heroin. Cut to her moving out of my apartment with a black eye that she'd received from getting hit by chunks of my puke. That's my biopic, because in real life, things keep going, and that's what inevitably happens when it comes to me.

I've had a few perfect moments when I wish the credits would have rolled and the film had ended. One that really stands out is the time I got a blow job from a porn star on the beach in front of the Delano Hotel in Miami at 5:00 a.m. It was February, when Florida has perfect, breezy weather. I can't say who the porn star was, but I can say that she was once on *Stern*, so we knew each other, and she wanted to get back on to promote something.

This happened when I went missing, which is something *Stern* fans will remember. I'd checked myself out of rehab and a few days later called in to the *Stern Show* from that hotel in Miami. What I didn't mention that morning was what had happened the night before.

When I walked into the Delano bar, she screamed my name at the top of her lungs. She was entertaining some guys who were fawning over her, but they were *Stern* fans, so when they saw me they really lit up. They started quoting stories I'd told on the air and jokes from my stand-up special. A few other people recognized me too, and I could tell that she got wet every time it happened. I had money on me, so I was buying people drinks, and she loved that. I told her to look me up on celebritynetworth.com because they say I'm worth way more than I am. As I've mentioned, that site lists what I should have, which back then was even more, about $14 million.

My salaries are public knowledge, so if you add them up, I should be worth $14 million. But what's not public knowledge is how much Bobo collected from me when I missed the over and under on the Holy Cross–Ramapo game in 2006. Nobody at celebritynetworth.com factored that in or who I bet to win the 2007 NCAA basketball tournament or how Virginia Tech did in the 2008 tournament. They really should have fact-checked with Bobo when he was still with us. I would have been happy to give them his number.

"What'd you say Artie is supposed to be worth?" he'd ask. "Fourteen mil? Hold on, me and my sons will do the math for you so you get this right. You didn't factor in that Villanova-versus-Georgetown game, I guess, because you're off by a little bit. According to our figures, he's worth about eighty grand. While I've got you on the phone, would you like to know my net worth for your website? I'm worth about $18 million, $13,920,000 of which is Artie's."

Anyway, I was talking to this beautiful porn star, and I'm no good with women, but by that point it was teed up. She was drinking, and she'd given me some sort of pill, just shot me this sexy look and laid it on my tongue, then laid one on hers. My God, was that great. Then we flowed onto the beach, and since I didn't have a rubber, she wouldn't fuck me, but that was even better. Why would I care about fucking her with a rubber when I could come in her mouth without one? Plus, this was a blow job from a porn star! A true professional! It was perfect and efficient like Jiffy Lube changing the oil in your car with her as the one-woman pit crew.

"What's the problem here, sir? Oh, an erect cock? Let me handle this." *Baaaap!* "There you go; you're all set. This one's on the house. Just mention my website on the air."

She got her money's worth too; that blow job was so good that I mentioned her website about eight million times. I'd work it in constantly. Howard was fine with it, because I'd told him that if he heard me mention a chick's website on the air, he had to go with it, because I only did that because I'd gotten a blow job.

After it was over, the sun was starting to come up, and she snuggled up next to me, and I couldn't believe how soft her skin was. She was a young, hot, modern porn star, nothing like the ones I grew up on. Every '70s porn star looked like Captain Lou Albano. I used to wonder who was jerking off to that, because sometimes it was hard to tell Ron Jeremy from the chick he was fucking, since they were equally hairy.

My point is, that's where my film should have ended. No sequel, no bloopers, no alternate endings—just that. I should have gone from that beach into the afterlife, preferably in a painless manner. Up there, I'd see my dad, who would tell me, "Dude, you came in here perfectly," and I'd float around on a cloud getting high fives forever.

The best part was that it took place on the beach! I could go up to my room and didn't have to invite her up. I'd come, so the only thing I invited up that night was a cheeseburger. I was making money, I was on *Stern*, I had the next week off, and there I was lying on the beach after a blow job.

But no, my life continued, as it always does, and that's the problem. Daylight arrived, and she left to return to her life of fucking men she likes to fuck—who, unfortunately for her, couldn't get her on the biggest radio show in the world—and I went off and continued to be me. I did my disappearing act from the *Stern Show* for eight days and really screwed things up, but I'd left rehab, and let me tell you, the one thing I knew for sure was that I wasn't in any hurry to return. What sounds like more fun—group therapy or being Tommy Lee for a night? Sorry, Doc, I'm going to have to skip group today. Actually, I'm skipping tomorrow too. No, actually, I'm wrong. I'm skipping forever.

15

WHERE HEROES DARE

I remember being on a USO plane with Nick Di Paolo, heading to Afghanistan to entertain our troops and wondering how we were going to sleep, because USO planes aren't exactly Emirates. They're decommissioned B-1 bombers, bare-bones military transport. The seats recline but not a lot, and I hate flying. Nick had brought one Ambien and slept like a baby for twelve hours. I hated him. I sat there watching him sleep and counted the ways I hated him. He didn't even take the whole thing. Before he knocked off, he gave me half of it, thinking he was doing me a favor. With my tolerance, I'm lucky if half an Ambien puts the big toe on my right foot to sleep. I ended up with a sore back and a headache, and for twelve hours I sat there wanting to strangle Nick to death in his sleep.

"What is he, an eleven-year-old Girl Scout?" I mumbled to myself. "Half an Ambien and he's snoring like Rumpelstiltskin."

But I forgot all about that the moment we landed, because I had been looking forward to giving back to my fans in the US military for a while. I'd sacrificed most of my vacation time from *Stern* to do the ten-day trip, which meant a lot, because, being allergic to mornings, nothing meant more to me than time off when I was on *Stern*. I'd invited Nick, Dave Attell, and Jim Florentine, all great comics. At the last minute, I added Gary Dell'Abate as our emcee. I met so many brave, dedicated, smart, and thoughtful soldiers, people who had families and loved ones at home, who treated what would scare most of us to death as nothing more than their day job. The training, the mental focus, the stamina it takes for them to keep their wits about them while they look out for each other—and, by extension, every single US citizen—is truly awe-inspiring to me.

What I also realized after one hour of being on the ground was that the brave men and women of the US military are the greatest risk takers I've ever met. Talk about life in the fast lane; they put theirs on the line, going all-in, every single day that they serve. To do that, you need faith. Someone like me has faith in the peace I experience from chaos and the sense of calm I get from the unpredictable. Die-hard gamblers have faith in luck, their instincts, or their skill at cards. The military personnel I met have faith too; they put blind faith in the orders handed down by the commander in chief, no matter what they are. If the president tells them to do something, they do it. They question nothing; they simply go out and do. A lot of Hollywood liberals are offended by people like that, but who do you want in your military—people like Ryan

Seacrest's assistant? You need warriors in an army, and warriors don't question orders.

Each of us had a personal bodyguard for the entire trip, because a few of the bases on the tour were in hostile territory. My bodyguard was a black marine from Brooklyn who spoke real ghetto and made fat jokes nonstop. I had to laugh at those, mostly fake laugh, because his job was to protect me, and I figured he'd do a better job if I seemed to like his jokes. At one point we were under mortar attack, and I asked him what would happen if I were to be hit by a mortar.

"Aw, man, don't worry about that at all," he said. "If one of those motherfucking things hits you, you're just gonna be dust. You'll disintegrate. You won't feel shit, so why worry about it?"

"Really?"

"Yeah, really. You get hit with a mortar, you gonna be dust. You of all people, you gonna be a lotta dust. And me, I'll have to clean up that dust, so have an apple for lunch today, you fat fuck."

I liked that kid so much; I had real affection for him. He was a good guy, with a wife and kid at home, and we had a lot of laughs, and for that reason, I purposely have not checked to see if he is still alive. I told him to look me up and call me if he ever needed anything, and I've found that most guys I've met in the military or the police or fire department that I say that to do call me at some point. It's been a few years, and it concerns me that I haven't heard from him, so I hope he's all right and that he knows I'm here if he ever needs me.

It would affect me if I found out that he died, because

even though it was only ten days, it seemed like an eternity. We were friends by the end, and it would really suck
to hear that he had died over there. Those guys see a friend
die, most of the time right next to them, and they have to
keep moving. A lot of times they have to leave them where
they fall because if they don't it will cost more lives, maybe
even their own.

I wanted to give the troops a great show, so when I was
invited by the USO, I purposely chose three guys who are
hard to follow, knowing that I would be closing every
night. Dave, Nick, and Jim are headliners all famous for
destroying, and everybody killed every show. In ten days,
nobody had a bad set. Attell set the tone on the very first
night. We were told that we couldn't do jokes about the
commander in chief, who at the time was George W.
Bush. That wasn't going to be a problem, because there
was not a liberal pussy among us. The other rule was no
masturbation jokes. I guess masturbating is an epidemic
over there. "Don't rile them up," is what the USO officer
told us.

Here's how Dave Attell opened his set and our tour.

"Listen," he said, "they told us that we can't talk about
masturbating with you. They said it was a rule, and I'm not
gonna break it. I'm a good citizen and I support our troops
in every way, so I will adhere to that rule and won't do any
jokes about masturbating. What I would like to do is open
up with a story about the time I was fucking a sock filled
with shampoo." He got a five-minute standing ovation,
but you should have seen the look on the face of the marine
in charge of our safety. He was standing stone still, shaking his head, as if to say, "You motherfucker." I'd like to

think I'd be the guy to do that, but I'm not. Dave Attell is. To me, that would be too much of a risk, because it wasn't the club owner at the Saint Louis Chuckle Hut laying down the law; it was the US fucking Army.

Anyway, by the end of our tour, we had done all the shows that were scheduled when the USO officer in charge told us that there was one last base where we could perform. It hadn't been mentioned when the trip was set up, because the USO had never arranged for any entertainers to visit it. The location was classified, deep in a remote region of Afghanistan, and all the troops stationed there were running black ops. It was off limits for A-listers like Billy Crystal because of the danger, but I guess we were special, by which I mean C-list. They told us it was very bare bones, so not to expect much, but they'd have a makeshift stage. They asked us to shorten our sets to about ten minutes and then spend the rest of the time just hanging out and talking with the guys for a while.

I immediately agreed, because I was happy to give them a break from their lives any way I could. They asked me to go because I'm single with no kids—low risk. I actually chose Attell and Florentine for the tour because neither of them have kids. If a tour I booked left a friend's kids fatherless, I'd never be able to live with myself. I tried to keep Gary Dell'Abate from coming on the trip at all because he's got a family, but he persisted until I eventually caved and let him be our emcee. That was fine, but I still think it was stupid for him to visit that black ops base. He actually said he was going to hang back, and then at the last minute, he got on the second helicopter, that motherfucker. I got into an argument with him when we arrived, because to me, he was risking his life for what? A story to tell Howard on the air?

We flew over the Afghan desert in a Black Hawk helicopter escorted by two Apaches, and we saw the caves and little foxholes in the sand where the Taliban live. The ground below would look like smooth sand, and then they'd just emerge from these holes with their wives and kids; it was completely insane. We also flew right over the ruins of Alexander the Great's castle, which was amazing to see.

We got there in the afternoon and waited, because the guys were delayed returning from an operation—and one of them wasn't coming back. I asked if we should just cancel since they'd lost a solider, but the troops didn't want that; they told their superiors that they needed to laugh now more than ever. There were chairs for about twenty guys, and eight of them decided to come see the show while the others got some rest. Those eight came in covered in dirt, and some looked like they'd been crying. They threw down their bulletproof vests and gear, slumped in their chairs, and stared at the stage with expressions unlike any I've ever seen in my life. They were looking for something, anything, to transport them back home, for a few minutes.

All of us went pretty low-key with our acts because the laughter threshold was at a minimum. Killing in that crowd was a chuckle, or one of them holding their gut and half laughing, looking like they were in pain. We adjusted and we did our thing, and when we finished, the amount of affection they showed us was unbelievable. We got so many sincere hugs. One of them said it best when he said,

"We're all hurting a lot right now, but you were so funny, that laughter really helped us out. I didn't think it would, but it did."

They told us about the friend they'd lost that day: his name, where he was from, and stories about him. A few started crying, and it was really rough, but I'm glad we were there with them. We signed autographs, we shared a meal together, and then they had to get to sleep, because they had to get back at it the next day.

During the return flight in the Black Hawk, I was allowed to shoot the huge gun mounted in the helicopter. The soldier who let me do it was a bit of a redneck.

"Artie, you want to shoot this fucker? You ain't never gonna get your hands on one of these again."

"Yeah, sure," I said. "But is there anyone out there? What if I actually kill some Taliban guy?"

"Shit, Artie, I hope you do. That will be one less I have to kill!"

Good thing I never wanted to be a sharpshooter, because there was a mountain directly in front of us and I couldn't hit it. I held off on telling my mother about any of this, because she didn't even want me to go fishing when I was a longshoreman, because she thought that I'd fall overboard and drown. This was a few clicks past fishing, but there was no way I was sitting that one out. I had to do what I could for guys who were gambling with their lives at the high-stakes tables.

What is their risk for, by the way? All we've done being over there is make things worse. There is a haunting piece of footage of George H. W. Bush during the first Gulf War talking about whether we should go all the way and take out Saddam Hussein. He says that we've taken the city, we've secured the oil we wanted, and that everything was under control. "If we take him out," he says, "what then?" It's too bad that thought never crossed the mind of his dumb, Bible-thumping son. Tell you what, we're finding out what "what then?" is right now. In Afghanistan, we created ISIS, and there is no bigger irony in the world.

No matter how much we spend and how many troops we send, we can't keep the place stable. We destroyed their capital and can't rebuild it fast enough; their kids are starving and now they hate us, and you can't blame them for that. We can't protect them from the Syrian rebels who come in and organize all that hatred. They gather people in town squares and make speeches and pass out literature to focus that fury. The outrage festered, and a decade later ISIS emerged. The "what then?" Bush Sr. was worried about became ISIS. They detest us so much that ISIS has people signing up, willing to die just to kill some of us and disturb our way of life. That's hatred on a level we do not understand here. I mean, I hate the Mets, but I wouldn't blow myself up to kill David Wright.

What I'm getting at is that when I look at the mess in Afghanistan, I see gamblers and risk takers on both sides. I see our troops risking their lives to protect our country and our way of life, and I see terrorists who are gambling big. When they play the right hand, with a nothing bet, they can seriously disturb life in the nations they consider their enemies. I hate to say it, but if you can motivate people to kill themselves to hurt the opposition, your strategy is working. Listen, I hate the Kardashians, but I'm not willing to kill myself to blow up Caitlyn Jenner. Actually, you know what? If I could get a guarantee that Scott Disick would die, I'd be willing to die. That's how strong my hatred of the Kardashians is. And what then? For my sacrifice, I hope someone would erect a statue of me, preferably on the beach in front of the Delano Hotel in Miami, to honor the fact that I prevented Scott Disick from procreating again.

16

SOME RISKS ARE TOO GREAT

The greatest actor I've ever worked with, hands down, is Laurie Metcalf. The multiple Emmy winner is known for her roles on *Rosanne*, *The Big Bang Theory*, *Toy Story*, and more. She is an original member of Chicago's famous Steppenwolf Theatre Company along with talents like John Malkovich and Gary Sinise. She was also Norm's costar on *Norm*, and I was lucky enough to have had many scenes with her during the two seasons I was on. On the show, her character hated mine and would get annoyed and hit me, so all I had to do was stand there and let Laurie be funny. She was hilarious, the perfect combination of timing, delivery, and physical comedy; meanwhile, everyone thought I was being funny. People would tell me that I was hysterical, and I'd say thanks and take the compliment, but it was all Laurie. I need to thank her, because her acting definitely got me laid a couple of times for my work on *Norm*. She's an amazing person, and she and I became great friends working on that show. Laurie also played my mother in *Beer League*, which was an enormous favor.

During the summer break between the second and what would be the final season of *Norm*, Laurie took a trip to the East Coast with her oldest daughter, Zoe, to look at colleges. I wasn't on *Stern* yet, but I already knew Gary Dell'Abate well, so I was able to get Zoe a summer internship there. Laurie was very grateful for that and asked me to go to lunch with the two of them to thank me. At the time, John C. Reilly and Philip Seymour Hoffman were doing the play *True West* at the Circle in the Square Theatre on Broadway. Laurie had front-row tickets because of her Steppenwolf pedigree, so we planned to see it after lunch and go backstage to say hello to Reilly and Hoffman.

The show was incredible. The play is about two brothers, and those two amazing actors would do two performances a day and switch roles for the second one. They'd do a matinee as one character and then play the other character in the evening. There is only one other character in the play, their mother, which Laurie played in a production of it when she was in her twenties, wearing makeup so that she'd appear to be an old woman. So she had a special attachment to *True West*.

When the curtain came down, we went backstage, and Laurie and her daughter caught up with John C. Reilly because they're friends. Philip Seymour Hoffman was there too, so he and I started talking.

"Wow," I said, "the show was really amazing, man. I can't believe you do two of those a day and change roles."

He was very down to earth, very humble, friendly, and

reserved. After a while, Reilly left with his girl, and Laurie and her daughter got ready to head out. Hoffman and I were the only ones with no plans.

"What are you doing right now?" he asked me.

"Nothing at all," I said.

"You want to get a steak with me?"

"Yeah, sure."

We went to a steak house nearby, I don't remember which one, and hung out for the next two hours. He was everything people say he was: thoughtful, intelligent, well-read. He hadn't won the Oscar yet—*Capote* was coming out the next year—but he was so clearly gifted, it was a privilege to spend casual time like that with him. He talked about acting the way great musicians talk about music, both aware and in awe of it. At the beginning of lunch, everything was great, but as the meal went on, I could see that he was sweating more than anyone should have been in that air-conditioned restaurant. By the end, he was in a rush to leave. I wasn't familiar with the symptoms then, but I sure am now. He had to get to his hotel room to get high and fend off the withdrawals so he could do the second performance.

When Philip Seymour Hoffman died, they found seventy bags of heroin and a pile of needles in the room. That's how much you buy when you want to be sure you have enough to keep withdrawals at bay, and that is a living hell. If you're traveling, you must be sure that at the other end of the plane ride, you either have some waiting or know where to get it, because if you don't, sheer panic sets in. It makes every single detail of flying a waking nightmare. And that's how it is if your plane leaves on time. If you're grounded by weather in an unfamiliar city, forget it; there isn't a first-class lounge in the world that has what you need on their list of amenities. It would be great if they did. "Welcome to American Airlines platinum lounge. We have massages, manicures, china white, cocktails, and dinner from five a.m. to ten p.m. daily."

Withdrawals are hell. I can't even imagine the anxiety Hoffman must have experienced doing that play. I've done stand-up routines in full-blown withdrawals, which I've come to affectionately refer to as my withdrawal sets. I'll never forget one that took place in Orlando, Florida. I was contracted to do an hour set for $60,000, and half an hour in, I realized I wasn't going to make it. I continued my act while trying to figure out how long I had until the uncontrollable diarrhea began. After the profuse sweating begins, the next phase is uncontrollable diarrhea.

If I shit my pants onstage, I wondered, *is that worse than leaving the stage early?*

It was a gamble, but I decided to keep going, and I nearly made it too. The very moment I left the stage, I started to shit my pants. If I'd been wearing a diaper, it would have been full by the time I got to the dressing room door. But I wasn't, so the shit just ran down my leg. As I often did in those days, I told my former assistant, Teddy, to get me new pants. By then he'd stopped asking why and had learned to find pants wherever we happened to be. If you ever find yourself applying for a job as my assistant, know now that "ability to find pants anywhere" is a prerequisite for consideration.

When I spent that afternoon with Philip Seymour Hoffman, I'd tried opiates once or twice, but never often enough to get hooked. Everyone's tolerance is different, but the commonly held rule of thumb is that you need to do them for about four days straight to become physically addicted, and I'd always pulled up short of that. After I crossed that line and got in too deep, I often replayed that lunch in my mind, seeing details of his behavior for what they really were. Even with that knowledge, and knowing how it ended for him, I still went for it. I needed more risk in my life at the time, and opiates are one hell of a way to put everything that matters to you at risk in one shot.

The morning after Hoffman died in 2014, both the *Post* and the *Daily News* ran pictures of him looking terrible: hair disheveled, unshaven, clothes a mess. I was headlining Caroline's that night, and here's how I opened.

"Guys," I said, "for once I didn't need a mirror this morning. You know why?"

I held the *Post* up next to my face, and the place went nuts. It was the biggest laugh I got all night, one that went right into a collective groan, because it was the darkest laugh ever. Then a drunk guy in the front yelled, "Faggot!" which, if you've ever been to Caroline's on a Friday, is pretty typical.

Whenever I struggle with heroin, I think of that lunch. I also think of the time back in 1998 that Mitch Hedberg, Greg Giraldo, and I played the Comedy Cellar and then went to the Chelsea Square Restaurant on Ninth Avenue and Twenty-third Street and talked until 7:00 a.m. If you took a picture of that table and had to choose the two guys who wouldn't be alive fifteen years later, I'm pretty sure I would have been one of them. It amazes me that I'm still here.

That night, we talked about everything, and you bet your

life we talked about dope. Mitch told us, as he told Dave Attell and other close friends of his, that he knew exactly what he was doing and knew how it would end.

"Guys, don't try to stop me," he said. "I love you for it and thanks for caring, but I'm doing heroin until the day I die. I'm going to shoot heroin every day until that happens, and nothing is going to stop me. Even if I get busted, I won't stop. I hear you can get it in jail pretty easy, so I'll just keep doing it there."

He'd bought a big Winnebago by that point so he wouldn't have to fly as much, and eventually that is where he and his wife lived full-time. He stopped flying altogether after he was stopped by customs officers and arrested because of a strange odor coming from him, which was gangrene. He'd shot up between his toes so much that his foot was rotting and was in such bad shape that he had to get half of it amputated. Two weeks later he died. He limped into the *Stern Show* studio the last day I saw him.

Greg Giraldo's demons might have been worse than Hedberg's, believe it or not. He wasn't shooting junk, but he was a self-fulfilling prophecy, because he thought it was rock and roll to do a lot of drugs. He also used to proudly say that comics were the new rock stars.

"All music sucks now," he'd say. "There are no new rock stars. Comics are the new rock stars. We are like AC/DC and Boston."

"Whatever, man," I used to say. "Now if that ain't the dope talking."

But he made an interesting point. When we were growing up, there were rock stars, but after Kurt Cobain, there really weren't any anymore. Some of the hip-hop guys filled the void, and guys like Eminem are great storytellers (he's like a hip-hop Springsteen, in my opinion), but they're few and far between. The last time I cared about buying music was in the mid-'90s. I remember going to buy *In Utero* the day it came out. After Cobain died in 1994, there was a shift, and I do think comedians filled that void. My generation of comics—Hedberg, Attell, me, Louis C. K., Dave Chappelle, Greer Barnes, and a few others—we tell stories, we reflect our times, and we push the envelope. And all of us got our big breaks right around the time Kurt Cobain died. I landed on *Mad TV* in '95, Attell hit that same year, and Hedberg hit big in '97. By the time show biz caught up to his genius, he was already burned out, however. When Comedy Central finally gave him a one-hour special, he tanked. It wasn't his fault, because the jokes were hilarious, but the audience sucked. If you watch it, you'll see Mitch telling amazing jokes and the audience sitting there confused because they don't get it. It's an important piece of history, because to me, that moment was the start of the politically correct, millennial bullshit that has stalled the evolution of stand-up comedy. Younger comics just don't take risks. The only upside of it all is that people like me who aren't afraid to "go there" in their material are outlaws. And show me a time in history when outlaws haven't been popular.

I'm lucky to have found my forum before all of that happened. I was able to do politically incorrect humor on a national level every morning for eight years behind a superstar radio host. Jeff Ross always says that the roasts he's now famous for were his Yankee Stadium. Dave Attell says his show *Insomniac* was his Yankee Stadium. Howard

was mine. And good thing, because Howard's show today
is the perfect example of how political correctness has ruined comedy. His show is so unbelievably safe, boring, and
just bad. It's amazing how sensitive people are today and in
being so, more narrow-minded, all under the guise of being more open-minded and accepting. They're accepting of
what they think is acceptable, which is the exact opposite
of being truly accepting and open-minded.

What I have come to accept is that there is one thing I
wish I could undo in my life. I'm not one to look at the
past with regret. Even if you haven't read my other books,
by this page you should realize that my ups and downs are
who I am, so I couldn't change much. Except for heroin.
That changed everything for me. It was the bet I wish I'd
never placed, the one chaotic demon I wish I hadn't invited into my life. It's the one high I wish I'd never known,
because it's the one you never quite capture again but
spend the rest of your life chasing. It is a cheap shortcut to
the kind of excitement I like, and one I wish I'd never discovered, because if you ask me, there are so many more
rewarding ways to make your life unstable, like quitting a
well-paying job to become a comic.

Opiate addicts are not like other people. There are more
than 30 million opiate abusers worldwide, with about 2.1
million here in the United States, half a million of which
are heroin abusers. Certain people, who may or may not
have tastes for other drugs, are simply wired for opiates,
and once they try them, that's a wrap. And it's not just
people whose lives are being devastated by them. It's parrots too.

In places like Neemuch, India, poppy farmers have

reported that a growing percentage of the parrot population in the area is addicted, and the parrots have been plundering their fields to satisfy their cravings. The birds wait until March and April when workers split open the flower pods, allowing them to ripen in the sun and produce morphine. The parrots will swoop down in silence, nibble the stalks just below the pod, then retreat to the high branches of a tree to enjoy their prize. These parrots have learned not to squawk or attract any attention while they make off with the flower pods. They will gorge on the poppy, up in the treetops, then sleep for hours. Some of them get so high that they nod off and fall to their deaths. It's the equivalent of falling asleep on the couch with a lit cigarette, which can be lethal if you don't live with someone like my podcast producer and roommate, Dan Falato, who is handy with a fire extinguisher.

This phenomenon was first reported a few years ago—by a parrot, I imagine—and it has become worse with each passing year. The farmers are losing about 10 percent of their crop to these junkie birds, which is a problem, because poppy farming is regulated by the Indian government and the farmers aren't making their quotas. If anyone wants to buy me a birthday present, by the way, I'll take a one-way ticket to Neemuch for spring break, and don't worry about getting me the international roaming plan, because I won't be needing my phone.

Anyway, the news reports I've read focus on the farmers in this situation, but what they're neglecting is the plight of the parrots. I've done some of my own research and found an interview with a Neemuch parrot who claims that once he got hooked on the poppy, he started to hate Jimmy

Buffett. His friends reported that he started playing guitar around that time and that he learned the solo from "Gimme Shelter" in under ten minutes. The parrots that eat poppy also seem to enjoy Charlie Parker more than the parrots who don't.

There are also the parrots who avoid the poppy and look on as their friends and neighbors dive down into the fields for their fix. They sit on branches beside them as the druggie birds nod off, and they watch some of them die, either from predators they are too high to avoid or by falling to their deaths. I'm no ornithologist, but it seems to me that the parrots who stay off the pop see the risk and choose to avoid it, despite how much better their friends are at guitar. I'm sure it's tempting, but those parrots don't want to end up sucking cock for poppy. And I can't blame them.

My point is that even animals can recognize opiate risk, but somehow at fifty years old, I can't. And that's because I'm a risk addict. Just look at me, still getting arrested for heroin and cocaine possession at my age, this latest time in the parking garage of my apartment building! How pathetic is that? I forgot my keys and got locked out of my apartment, Dan was away, and I had an hour to kill before a locksmith could show up. I'd just come back from picking up a significant amount of drugs, because there's nothing worse than running out, so it was all there. But my point is this: rather than wait in the lobby of my building, or even in one of the many restaurants near my house, I decided to wait in my car, in my garage, and get high. It was stupid, because looking the way I usually do, which is somewhere just north of vagrancy, one of my neighbors assumed that I had broken into my Range Rover, and called the cops. They didn't think it could be mine; they thought I was in there sleeping or shitting. I was doing both, actually, and legally, because it was my car. Anyway, I was arrested, and my love of opiates put all that I had going for me in danger once again. The only upside when something like that happens is that while some call it "tragic," Anthony and I call it "a chapter."

If I could go back to the '90s when I was on blow and my life was chaotic, I would. You can stop snorting blow if you want to, you can stop smoking weed, but heroin and opiates of any kind become a part of you. They become your oxygen. You might think you're invincible, but play around with them and in no time, you'll have a serious habit to the point that you'll need them every eight hours. That's what these poor parrots don't understand. If I could speak parrot, I'd tell them that one day they're going to come back to the field and the poppies will be gone. There will be panic in parrot park. I'd ask them, "What the fuck will Polly do then?"

Whether you're a bird or a person, withdrawals are horrible, but I'm not sure anyone into opiates thinks it's that bad until it happens to them. If I were a farmer in Neemuch, I'd try to make that point to those poppy-eating parrots. Since language would be an issue, I'd probably organize a screening of *Sugar Hill* for them, which is a pretty bad movie from 1993, aside from how well Clarence Williams III, star of the hit '70s TV show *The Mod Squad*, recreates withdrawals. He has a scene where he gets a hot shot, which is a deliberately lethal dose of heroin, from his son, who is a heroin dealer, and dies. But before he ties himself off for the last time, he gives a speech about the first time he did heroin. He's in full withdrawal, sweating, and it's so convincing that I can barely watch it. Seems to me that Clarence might have had some real-life experience, if you know what I mean. Anyway, his character tells his son that if he's selling, he can never start using, because it will never let him go. Then he tells a story and delivers a line that would be cheesy coming from a lesser actor: "I was on my way to church, and my dealer stopped me and said, 'Son, where are you going? This is your God!'" He pulled that line off. Black people can do that with language. Think of a white guy doing that line; it would be terrible. Quincy Jones used to call me a "funny cat." That was cool as hell coming from him. If someone like Ryan Seacrest said that to me, I'd want to hit him with a fungo bat.

Heroin is the ultimate risk. And being the loser I am, I had to try it. I survived cocaine, pills, and gambling, I made it through my crazy youth and early career in show business, and when the smoke cleared, I was on *Stern* and earning a hundred grand a weekend doing stand-up. I'd gotten my dream job: telling stories about my friends and me as kids and getting laughs and being paid for it. I did imitations of a cartoon rooster, of Foghorn Leghorn, on the radio for millions of people. Back in high school when I'd get in trouble for disrupting class doing that imitation, I was told that I'd never use that skill. Well, I did, Mr. Mafucci—just thought you'd like to know! Clearly, being on *Stern* was the only job I was ever cut out to do.

But I needed to fuck that up. I like getting high, and I'd done every drug except heroin. How could I resist? That one came with the risk of getting hooked pretty quickly. I decided to try it once, and if I could go back to that night in that hotel room, I'd tackle myself. I snorted some china white, and to this day I've never had anything so pure in my life again. It might have just seemed that way because it was my first hit, but I don't think so. I tell this story in my first book, but I will never forget what happened after I did those first two lines. It was around 3:00 a.m., and I lay back on the bed and said aloud, before my head hit the pillow, "I'm in trouble." I still am. I've chased that high ever since, all the way into my garage not long ago. It has not been worth it, but when you're an opiate addict, you don't realize that until it's too late.

I'm going to get serious here for a minute, because the opiate epidemic in this country has reached outrageous proportions. More than 50,000 people died of drug overdoses in 2015, which is higher than auto accidents, and for the first time in US history, more than those killed by gun violence. And it's only getting worse. This didn't happen overnight; it happened because opioid prescriptions have tripled since 1990, jumping from 76 million to 219 million prescriptions for painkillers written by doctors in 2011. That's insane! All those people can't always get pills, so what has also increased is the demand for heroin, which is cheaper than pills if you're buying on the street. What we've seen as a result is a massive increase in heroin production in Mexico and South America and more lethal overdoses in younger age groups, across all races, than ever before. Actually, whites and Native Americans lead the charge there, but according to a report in *The New York Times*, that's because doctors are more reluctant to prescribe painkillers to minority patients, because they're worried that they might sell them or become addicted.

I'm getting all these facts from an in-depth report by *Frontline*, which airs on PBS, by the way. This isn't fake news.

I bring this up because there is only one way to turn this disaster around, and it's a difficult one, because there is money involved. All of this happened because doctors started overprescribing, and why did that happen? Because they get kickbacks from the pharmaceutical companies. They get free trips, they get to have free dinners with the smoking-hot drug reps who come to their offices to drop off the newest pills, then they write scripts for those pills and eventually end up with yachts. Doctors need to stop that bullshit and start being honest with their patients, especially their youngest ones.

Say you're a seventeen- or eighteen-year-old kid who comes in with an injury. Maybe the kid has seen Artie Lange do an offensive joke on YouTube while he was home in his safe space, and ever since, he's had trouble breathing, because his heart is bruised by what he saw. Or let's say a kid hurts his elbow while playing football. What doctors have been saying too often in the past twenty years is, "Your elbow hurts? Take some OxyContin and get some rest." The doctor equates fixing the pain with fixing the situation.

The kid gets a bottle of fifteen OxyContin, and he takes them and he feels pretty damn good, because the injury isn't that bad in the first place. So when the bottle is empty, he wants another. When you're exposed to substances, opiates especially, before your midtwenties, there is a statistically greater chance that you will become addicted. So our kid with the hurt elbow goes through his bottle of fifteen pills, and even though the injury isn't bothering him anymore, he tells his parents and his doctor that it is, because he wants to keep getting high. The doctor has given him two refills, so he gets one and finishes it in half the time, because he's doubling up and enjoying himself, but by the time he gets through that second bottle, he's physically addicted.

For most people, this is where their lives go off the rails. This is a common scenario that puts kids out of commission for at least a little while, if not permanently. Our guy's hopes of being on the football team for the rest of the season are over, as is wanting to get out of bed in the morning. He's in withdrawals at seventeen, not knowing what the fuck is going on. If his parents know nothing about drugs, they'll just think he's sick. So they get him his last refill, which he goes through in just a few days because he's tripling up now, and the doctor won't give him another refill, because that would be bad doctoring and could cost him his medical license. Or maybe he's unavailable because he's yachting.

There's nothing funny about this, because it's par for the course in our country these days. In the past twenty years, doctors have become drug dealers, especially when it comes to kids. If a seventeen-year-old gets a sports injury, chances are it will be better in a few days at most—because the kid is seventeen! Instead, the injury is replaced with a desire for something that the kid didn't even know existed just a short time before.

Once the kid has the taste, he will never lose it. He'll be at a high school party with his dicklick friends, and he'll ask around. He'll be able to tell who has the pills on them, believe me. They will be drug dealers, who may be white with long hair or fellows of a darker complexion. And the drug users will be even easier to find, because they will look like me. They'll probably have something on their shirt that is either drool, throw-up, a cookie, or a leftover piece of OxyContin. It's rare, but one of them might even have a chronically bleeding nose from the time last month when he accidentally snorted Oxy mixed with glass.

In any case, this kid's football injury has transformed him into a statistic in no time. He's now one more kid who needs to be detoxed, all because of a hurt elbow. It simply wasn't like that not long ago. That could have never happened to me at seventeen, because there was only weed and blow going around when I was a kid, never opiates or other prescription drugs. If that had happened to me at seventeen, I'd be dead. I meet kids in my NA and AA meetings all the time that look at me and think I've somehow made it through life successfully as a junkie. That could not be further from the truth, and I make sure to let them know. I wasn't a teenage junkie; I made my bones in the business before I got into it. I started in my midthirties, when I had money.

These poor kids nowadays, I really feel for them, because they are going through some horrible shit. I went to an AA meeting in Pittsburgh that was single-handedly the most depressing gathering I've ever been to in my life. This was after the zipper-nose incident, by the way, so I was already feeling pretty terrible and looking even worse. But I came off more composed than George Clooney compared to these kids. At the end of the meeting, they were hugging me, saying that I inspired them and that if I could have made it to where I am in life being a junkie, then they could succeed too. "If you can do it, we can do it," they kept saying.

"No," I'd say, "you don't understand. I'm not doing it. This is not what it looks like when you're doing it."

Those kids I met were in a horrific place. Most of them were going home as junkies to a house where their parents were junkies too. Nearly all of them told similar stories about their parents stealing their drugs and leaving them to suffer the withdrawals. How awful is that? A family like that will eventually kill each other, be institutionalized, or be killed by other people. I can't think of a more desperate, hopeless situation. I've been in withdrawals that were so bad that if I weren't handcuffed to a bed with someone watching me and caring for me, I would have killed myself by jumping off the balcony the second I got loose. Since I've been a junkie, I've always had money, so unlike Robert Downey Jr.'s character in *Less Than Zero*, I've never had to blow a guy for drugs. But then again, Dan Falato never asked. We have had the following conversation, however:

"Dan, just drive to Washington Heights and pick up the envelope."

"I can't; I'm reading the *Architectural Digest*."

"What if I blow you?"

Dan might act like that little chat hasn't happened, but it has. It's better for both of us that he refused, but I'd like Dan and everyone else to think about how much worse it would be if I were in one of those junkie families. If I were, my father and I might both be blowing Dan for heroin, maybe even at the same time.

Anyway, doctors have been administering prescription pills with the discrimination of a Pez dispenser for the past twenty years, and now we have ghettos of drug addicts in the suburbs of cities like Pittsburgh and Philadelphia. Drugs used to be an inner-city problem, but now it's a suburban one thanks to the pharmaceutical companies and the doctors. Think about it: when cocaine was king, drug dealers used to look like Robert Loggia in *Scarface*. They had money and class, and even in the inner cities, they were pimps who drove Cadillacs. Now they're all white trash kids with mullets who cook meth when times get tough. They look like Michael Anthony, the bass player for Van Halen, but with half a nose because it's been blown off in a meth lab explosion. They're chubby rednecks with access to a shack where they occasionally make terrible meth and never clean the spackle buckets. And don't get me started on synthetic weed and all the other shit people are turning to because they're desperate once they lose access to the pills that got them hooked. That shit, whatever it is, needs to be stopped right away. It's turning people into zombies. Remember that one guy in Florida who was high on that garbage and bit someone's face off? And the guy who barreled through Times Square in his car, taking out crowds of people because he was high on it and heard voices? It's almost as if a foreign nation is waging chemical warfare on our population with that stuff. Thank goodness synthetic weed is produced in China, a country that has our best interests in mind.

What I'm getting at here is that doctors might be the only people who can turn this epidemic around. They need to focus on prevention rather than acting as the gateway to addiction. They have to nip this in the bud and be the vaccine for this disease, and here's how. There should be some sort of regulation and instruction that they get from the government out of the gate, plus repercussions if they prescribe pills to teenagers who don't need them. But most importantly, they need to take the time to talk to these kids and not be lazy and just give them a pill for the pain. No matter how hot the chick from Pfizer is, they need to sit the injured kids down and let them know what could happen. Doctors with shitty bedside manner can always just appeal to their macho.

"Listen, Rocco, I know your elbow hurts, but I need to ask you something."

"Okay, Doc."

"You seem like a tough kid. You hurt your elbow. You've got to tell me seriously how much it hurts. Sit and think about it. Can you get through tonight? Can you get through a bit of tomorrow the way it hurts right now?"

"I guess so. Yeah, I guess I could."

"I think you can. If you tell me you can't, I'm your doctor, I've got to help you out and give you a pill. And I will do that, but first I'd like to show you a short film about what could happen. It's called *Don't Be Artie Lange*."

If they don't like my humor, the doctor or even a nurse could read them an article about Mike Webster, the famous Super Bowl and All-Pro Pittsburgh Steeler who spent his post-football life hooked on drugs to deal with a multitude of symptoms and was dead by fifty. After that, I'm sure the kid will tough it out. And maybe the doctor won't get laid by the girl from Pfizer, but you know what? She wasn't going to fuck the doctor anyway. She was going home to her gym trainer husband the whole time. Put it this way: if she looked like Christie Brinkley, the doctor was only ever going to get some version of Christie's daughter, who looks like Billy Joel on the cover of *The Stranger*, by the way.

I know this sounds goofy and corny, but it's really simple: we have to be human beings watching out for each other, and it needs to start on the front lines with the doctors. They need a code of ethics when it comes to this stuff. And that, in my humble junkie opinion, is what needs to happen. That will help reverse the pill issue, which will, in turn, reverse the heroin problem. Those kids who can no longer afford the pills turn to Mexican brown, because it's so fucking cheap. I'm not using any proven frame of reference, but having a baggie delivered from Patterson, New Jersey, to, say, north Hoboken costs about eighteen bucks. Again, I'm guesstimating.

It's really sad that a chemical can bond to you and become a lure and a trigger for the rest of your life. A lure so strong that even parrots can't resist it. Yet still, even in the avian world there are those who have sense, who aren't degenerates. They're the ones who say, "Fuck that! Polly go to DeVry! Polly go to DeVry! Polly go sell bras and girdles! Polly go sell bras and girdles!" They don't say, "Polly get high and go to an open mic!"

I'm one of the idiots. I'm one of the people who thought taking huge risks made you cool. It really doesn't. That's the reason why I'm not *The King of Queens*. Well, not the only reason; Leah Remini hated me. My point is that I've seen certain people whom I know are less talented shoot past me on the career track. Maybe I'm wrong. My mother thinks I'm more talented than the people I'm thinking of, and that's very nice of her. I tend to agree with her when she says things like that.

But none of that matters anymore. By taking the biggest risk I could, the one that made me "cool," I paid the price. I couldn't get up early enough to make the auditions for *High Fidelity* and *School of Rock*. Somebody who was chubby did get up on time and made those auditions. One of us was an all-county baseball player in his day; one of us was not. None of that matters anymore, but while we're on the subject, I was also on heroin when the auditions were held for the role of the retard in *There's Something About Mary*. It's too bad, because I do a great retard. I do a high-functioning one every day, in fact. Listen, the point I'm trying to make, besides the doctors and the parrots, is that my ultimate risk cost me. I know that all my losses come back to the fact that I bet that I could beat addiction. I lost that bet. Trying out dope and getting hooked and chasing it ever since has characterized my life since my late thirties, and it hasn't been glamorous or fun. There are only two good things that have come out of it, which is why I'm writing this chapter at all: 1) helping kids to not do as I've done, and 2) about three hundred grand from my publisher.

17

IF YOU HIT, YOU PLAY

Uncle Artie was visited by an angel recently. The angel didn't have wings, wasn't white as the driven snow, and I'm not setting up a joke that involves someone Hispanic named Angel. That does remind me of a joke, though. Isn't it great when somebody tells you that Jesus loves you? His love knows no bounds. He loves you no matter what you've done. That's great to hear. Unless you're in a Mexican prison.

My angel was a bit different; he was a member of the LAPD, which is a miracle considering my past relationship with the LAPD, specifically the time I threw a wild haymaker at an officer after a footrace that started on the NBC lot, continued through a grocery store, and ended in the middle of a busy intersection. I had a giant bag of coke in my pocket when they caught me, which didn't help matters. I should have stashed that in aisle 3.

Anyway, I was in LA for the premiere of *Crashing*, which

was an exciting week. There was press and stand-up to do, and we screened the show and had a party at Avalon. I was so nervous that I left the screening early and went back to my hotel because I couldn't even watch it. Let's face it: the offers for featured roles on an HBO series aren't exactly rolling in, so I was worried sick that I'd done a terrible job and was about to bomb, never to be considered for TV again. This made sense considering how I'd prepared for shooting those episodes, running white lines with the Sexy Southie. So I left and sat alone in my hotel, a nervous wreck, until my sister called me to say that the show was great and that I'd done really well and that I should come and enjoy the party. I was happy to hear that, but I still wasn't going back. *She's my sister*, I thought. *Of course she's going to say that I did well.* Finally, Jimmy Kimmel called and told me to stop being ridiculous, that I'd killed and that everyone there wanted to see me. So I went back to Avalon, and Gina Gershon gave me a huge hug, and everyone I saw said that I'd done a great job. I took everyone's words with a grain of salt until I finally watched the premiere and the entire season a few days later. All I can say is that Judd Apatow is truly a genius, because he knew what to do with me. He knows how to get the best out of people, and he really knows how to work with stand-ups, which isn't easy. Judd got a great performance out of Dave Attell, Greer Barnes, and everybody else from my world who appeared in season 1. What I did on *Crashing* is the best work I've ever done on television, and I'm honored to be a part of it. And I have Judd to thank for it.

To coincide with the *Crashing* promo tour, Pete Holmes, Judd, and I also did stand-up gigs. The plan was for me to close each show, after Judd and Pete, and in New York, after Dave Attell. Judd and Pete attract a real alternative comedy crowd, which is a bit of a challenge for someone like me, and following Dave Attell, the greatest comic alive, is an incredibly tough test that I was looking forward to. Dave is my friend, but I told him not to hold back, because this was a big spot for him too. He destroyed, and then I went up and killed for an hour, which is not easy to do, but it happened. In my business, it's the equivalent of pulling a rabbit out of a hat, which is easier to do if your business is magic.

I'd killed in New York and I killed in LA, and after I saw the entire season of the show, I felt truly, deeply happy. Against the odds, it had all worked out. After days of nail-biting, Dan could finally take a breather, because he'd successfully seen me through my committments for the week. The poor guy was tired, so he went to get some well-deserved sleep in his hotel room. I told Dan that I was going to sleep too, but once I was alone I changed my mind and decided to take in the night air. The next thing I knew, I was across town at a bar that I used to frequent, and I wasn't going there to drink. At this particular establishment, there are guys in the back who sell things that are quicker than liquor. This particular place is where I first bought blow in LA back in 1996, and as of last February, business is still booming, because, let's face it, no one is going to win a war on drugs. When I got there, I recognized a bouncer that I'd met years ago, and he recognized me and he gave the guys in back a nod so they'd let me through the door, into the part of the bar I was interested in.

Now, I knew it was a bad idea for me to be there at all

and an even worse idea for me to buy drugs. But I knew why I was doing it: I'm a junkie who abhors boredom. And as fucked up as it is, that self-knowledge comes with a deluded sense of freedom. Plus, things were going so well that I had a reason to celebrate. To commemorate an achievement, some people pop bottles of champagne with their friends. I snort drugs alone in my room. I couldn't resist. But I had my head on my shoulders: I planned to have just a little bit of fun without throwing it all into the blender the way I had with the Sexy Southie. At the same time, just before I decided how much I was going to buy, I recalled something the famous producer Bernie Brillstein once said to me, and he'd told me that he'd said the same thing to both John Belushi and Chris Farley and often regretted saying it, even though it's true. He asked them, as he asked me, "What did you get into show business for? Was it not to fuck hookers and do drugs? Then you must want to be an accountant. I hear they're hiring." According to that philosophy, if you're in show business and not getting high and fucking a whore, then you're wasting your time. What an angle! It's a great one to use to fool yourself if you only have the one shot, like I did that night.

I bought myself coke and heroin and fell way off the wagon, and to be honest, I fucking enjoyed it. I'm not trying to justify my actions, but I did learn something new this time, which is saying a lot because doing drugs is something I've done far too often to find them enlightening anymore. As a lot of people know, opioids cause constipation, which is a big problem for everyone who abuses them. Junkies talk about this all the time, and no one seems to have figured out a way around it. Well, on this bender, I solved the riddle. I learned that if you do cheap, stepped-on Mexican coke, you will not get constipated when you do heroin. It simply doesn't happen. I wish I had known this years ago when I was a practicing junkie full-time; it would have made life so much easier. If you do coke when you do heroin, you just speedball all your problems right out of your ass.

Speaking of colon health, I've been enjoying one of the many TV ads aimed at 111-year-olds that Fox News airs every two minutes. If you weren't aware, humanity has taken another giant step forward and we now have at-home colon cancer test technology. Thanks to the miracle of science and UPS, you no longer need to leave your house to give your doctor a stool sample. You can now take a shit in a box in the comfort of your own home and have UPS pick it up. It's amazing what our society is capable of, and the best part of it all is that the entire experience is brown. You put your brown in a box and then Big Brown takes it away in a big, brown truck. Probably by a black guy, which, again, is more brown. The commercial is the funniest thing. It features a very pleasant, nonthreatening black gentleman, about sixty-eight, wearing a powder-blue V-neck sweater, sitting in his immaculate home, straight out of *Better Homes and Gardens*. The entire commercial is narrated by the animated box that you put your shit in if you use this service. The pleasant black guy is reading a magazine, but he is going to shit in the talking box. He goes in the bathroom, and the box says something like, "And I go with you. And you do your business in me!" The box keeps narrating, smiling and talking as it walks out of the bathroom, now full of the guy's shit. The box is smiling after the guy literally just shit into its head. The box then walks itself to the curb and gets picked up by Big Brown. It's unbelievable. It's almost as weird as the commercial for toe fungus medication that Mario Lopez does. There is a giant toe with fungus on it, wearing a top hat, talking to Mario Lopez. If you ask me, the fungus and the box of shit need to get together. They need a sitcom, like *The Brady Bunch*. "Here's a story . . . of a toe with fungus . . . who is best friends with a box that's full of shit . . ." Fridays! . . . After an all-new *Flimsy Shine*.

Anyway, I got my drugs and had enough sense to get out of there before I got into even more trouble. I went to an all-night restaurant that I like to get some food and get high before I locked myself in my hotel room. And that is when this bender taught me another lesson: I not only discovered that you don't get constipated if you do coke while doing heroin but also that you are able to eat if you do heroin while doing coke. It's all connected! This was a revelation.

After I finished my meal, I went to pay at the register up front just as two cop cars pulled up. It was about 4:00 a.m. and I looked like hell, just a disheveled mess, paying for my meal, all by myself. The cops came inside and ordered coffee, and one of them recognized me.

"Artie, how you doin', man?"

They were very nice, we made small talk, and they asked if I minded taking a picture with them, which of course I didn't.

"Let me just pay my bill, and we'll take a picture," I said.

I reached for my money, forgetting about all the drugs in my pocket, and as I handed the cashier some bills, a pile of heroin packets wrapped in rubber bands fell to the floor, landing at their feet. Like most all-night restaurants, the place was brightly lit, so there was no way they didn't see it. There was also no chance that I could stand on the baggies or kick them away because there were a lot of them. I had enough on me to do five years in jail.

One of the cops bent over and picked it all up. "What the hell is this shit?" he asked. "We're going to have to take you in."

The other cop was calm and cool. "Artie, I don't know what to do here, man," he said. "Possession? Everyone in this restaurant is watching us. Let's take this outside."

When we were standing in front of their cars, he turned to the other cop. "Just go. I'll handle this. Get out of here. And get rid of that." The other guy shot him a look, then threw the drugs down the nearest sewer and drove off.

It was lightly raining, and all that I could think about wasn't whether or not I was going to be arrested—it was that my heroin was ruined and that I'd have to go score, because if I didn't, I'd be going into withdrawals in a few hours. Even if the drugs weren't wet, I was still too fat to get down that sewer, and the bar where I'd bought the drugs was now closed. I was screwed.

The cop who stayed with me was older, in his late forties or early fifties.

"Hey, thanks a lot, man," I said. "I can't thank you enough for that. How much time you got in? You've got to be close to retirement."

"I've got a few years left," he said. "Listen, I've been on every side of this problem. Are you going to be sick?"

"Yeah, I am."

"Are you doing a show tomorrow?"

"Yeah."

"Well, what are you gonna do?"

"I don't know. I just know you guys did me the biggest favor. I could be in jail right now."

"Yeah, but what are you going to do?"

"I don't know. I'm going to be sick tonight," I said. "I guess I'll have to figure something out tomorrow."

"Do you have a connection out here?"

"Maybe I can find some, but it's going to be hard."

The guy looked at me, looked back at the people watching us, then said, "All right, come with me."

He grabbed my arms and put them behind my back.

"Make believe you're being handcuffed," he said. Then he put me in the back of the squad car and started driving toward downtown LA.

"You know," he said, "this is a testament to Howard, to the radio show, and to you, because I wouldn't do this for any other celebrity, and I've met a lot of celebrities. I wouldn't do this for the biggest star in Hollywood, not even Tom fucking Cruise."

"Well if you were helping Tom Cruise," I said, "we'd definitely be cruising, but not for heroin, that's for sure."

The guy laughed and we kept driving, and it occurred to me that I had no idea what was going on.

"Where are we going, man?" I asked. "What are we doin'?"

"How much do you think you need?"

"Well, I'm leaving Saturday, and I need to wean off of it."

We drove to a shitty area of downtown where there were kids outside on corners in spite of the rain, because people treat rain in LA the way they do blizzards everywhere else in the world. When the kids saw the cop car, they scattered, but he managed to grab one of them and shook him down and found packets of heroin on him.

"It's your lucky day, kid; get out of here," he said. Then he got back in the car, and we drove away.

"This is for you, Artie," he said and handed me the heroin. "Promise me you'll at least try to get help when you get home."

"I will, man, I promise. I can't believe how kind you're being to me. Do you want tickets for the show?"

"Hell yeah, I do."

"Okay, you'll have great seats, as many as you want."

"That's great, but I want you to promise me that you'll be careful. Stay away from that Fentanyl. It is killing people every single day."

"I will. I promise. I can't thank you enough, man. You don't know how much this means to me."

The first cop would have hauled me in, but because the second one was a fan, I managed to risk everything and get away with it. The moral of the story is: you hit, you play. People say that show business is forgiving, but it's not. It's ruthless at every level, so you only get a second chance if you're talented. Robert Downey Jr. was given that chance because he's great. Jeff Conaway from *Taxi* was not given that chance and died in a hospital bed. In my crazy, pigeonholed world, I can hit, so I get to play.

Take Michael Vick. He electrocuted and drowned dogs, and there is nothing more needlessly cruel that you could possibly do in the off-season. No one is going to give him a cameo in *Beethoven Goes to College*, but the NFL took him right back and Philly snapped him up without a thought. And that is because he's a great quarterback. He killed innocent, living things for no good reason, but that is excused in his world. Take Plaxico Burress, who shot himself in the leg in a nightclub with an unlicensed gun. He did two years in prison, and the day after he got out, he was running routes on a warm-up field. The next day, he was once again a wide receiver in the NFL. If he weren't great, he'd be working at a car wash.

In my case, show business is my enabler, because I can hit, so they let me play. The risks I take are my enablers too, which is even worse, because one day I'm going to get royally fucked in the ass. Actually, that happened already, when I lost my job on *Stern*, but time erased it and I was given yet another shot. Still, the love of risk and its strongest manifestation in my life, the love of dope, remains. That love is greater than the love of success or the thrill of achievement to me. If someone handed me a bank card and told me that there was $10 million in an ATM and that all I had to do was put the card in, enter the PIN, and withdraw it, here's what I'd do. First of all, that is a dream no one would expect to achieve, so already I'd be in fantasyland and on cloud nine. All I'd have to do is withdraw the money, but what would I do instead? I'd stop one foot in front of the ATM and try to throw the card into the slot. Why? Because it's more exciting! If I make that shot in an already unbelievable situation, this story becomes the greatest story of all time! What would probably happen is that I'd miss and my worst enemy would pick up the card, put it in, and leave with the money. But those moments leading up to my shot would be interesting, I promise you that.

Here's another way to look at it, and it involves Elvis. In

my opinion, Elvis got fat and started dressing like Liberace and doing kung fu moves onstage because getting pussy had become too easy for him. He was so famous and good-looking and talented that getting all that pussy was a chore. So what did he do? He made it interesting; he gave himself a handicap. He ate fried peanut butter sandwiches laced with pills until he'd gained eight hundred pounds. He started dressing like the doorman at a gay club and passing out on toilets. And still, he got laid. He had no choice but to get laid; that's how great he was.

In many ways, show business was too easy for me. I was a millionaire by twenty-nine, so I had to find a way to keep it challenging, because improbable odds are the only ones I've ever known. When I showed up to the *Crashing* set, fresh off a bender with a shredded, bleeding nose, Judd gave me the spiel about taking care of myself but also said that we would work around it. And we did, and somehow he got the best performance out of me that I've ever given on television. That's because he's great, but I needed to put myself at a disadvantage to be able to give him my best. I don't recommend this method, because it's not a choice; it's just how I work.

Judd and I have a real friendship partly because he has an affection for addicts and enjoys stories of artists overcoming their demons. Everyone wants to be something they're not, and I think he believes that he's had it too easy and that he got his break too early. Even though he's more successful and talented than I'll ever be, I think he feels that fuckups like me are more of an artist than he is. I don't agree; Judd is a master of comedy and television and everything he puts his hand to.

I am lucky that Judd feels that way, though, because if he didn't, he would have tired of my song and dance by now. He also would have been less understanding of the fact that when I got back to my hotel room with all that heroin, I got really high and continued to do so and was still too fucked up two days later to get on the plane to fly to San Francisco. It was a private plane too, so I'm talking fucked up. I told Judd why and everything that had happened, and he was okay with it. I wasn't happy that I let him and Pete and the fans down, but my night scoring drugs with the LAPD had been too insane. I had to get very high just to make sense of it. That cop knew everything I was about to go through, and he showed me mercy. It was the most spiritual deliverance that has ever happened to me. That guy was an angel. And what kind of angel gets you heroin? An angel from LA, I suppose. As I sank into my hotel sheets, I thought, *I can't believe I was wrong before. That wasn't it. A cop just copped me heroin.* Now *everything's happened.*

CONCLUSION

IS IT BLOOD
OR HAWAIIAN PUNCH?

Here we are at the end of the line, so it's time to take stock of what we've learned. This is where we ask each other what it's all about. I can't speak for you, but I've explored what it means to be addicted to thrills and allergic to boredom, and as destructive as it's been, I've enjoyed the ride. But here at the finish line, I'm not going to lie: I've got nothing. The only thing I know about being human is that there is no black and white, because however many ways I try to analyze my existence, that one thing never changes.

I've gone through so many ups and downs, most of them a side effect of my decisions, and through those trials and tribulations I've learned that I have a problem that I'm doing my best to live with every day. Look at me: I'm doing a lousy job, but I swear to God that I'm doing my best. This is a never-ending battle that will continue to rage inside my mind and soul 24-7 until the day I die. I'll never excuse my behavior, but what I try to do is understand it, and I've learned that many of my most important decisions haven't been made logically. Usually my actions are hurtful to everyone in my personal and professional lives no matter how much sense they make to me in the fleeting moments in which I make them. I'm doing my best to minimize that collateral damage so that I can enjoy all the gifts and second chances that I've been given. I want to silence the evil in me when it tells me to burn the motherfucker down. Some months I'm successful at keeping the wolves at bay, and some months I'm not. But I mean it when I say that I'll keep fighting the good fight, and I'll try to stay away from the kind of excitement and the kind of people that enable the bad in me. Even when I'm actively pursuing the wrong path, I never lose sight of the light at the other end of the tunnel. That is the blessing and the curse of knowing what makes you tick.

But I realize—and you should too so that you're not disappointed in me—that I'll always choose fun first. If the choice is health food or candy, I'll always choose candy at the most inopportune times, and my blood sugar reflects that. I'm sorry, guys, but I love fun, I love being bad, I love setting fires and playing pranks. I love making a fool of myself, even if I'm the only one in the room who gets the joke.

I'd like to leave you with one last tale, the one that inspired the working title of this book, which for legal reasons, is now the title of this chapter instead. It captures the essence of what it means to be me and to be a degenerate gambler, which in my case are one and the same.

When I was twenty, still working at Port Newark and in my heyday of enthusiastically betting, drinking, and snorting coke beyond the limits of my paycheck, I had a circle of friends that I'd hang out with doing the same. One buddy in particular, who we will call Tommy, was my partner in crime. Like Norm and me, Tommy and I were a real pair, driving each other to new heights of risk and new lows of degenerate behavior. All my friends in that crew liked all the same things, and we pursued our most self-destructive vices with gusto. We were young and making money and felt invincible, so every weekend was an adventure in depravity.

I was living at home, taking care of my mother, acting as the man of the house as much as I could, but since Tommy had his own place, I would hang out and crash there a lot. Tommy's was where all of us got together to watch games, get fucked up, and bet, so why would I want to be anywhere else? Tommy had a Mexican maid named Maria who cleaned his apartment every Monday. She did his laundry too, and since I felt guilty about having my mom clean my clothes with everything else on her plate, I used to bring my dirty clothes to Tommy's and give Maria twenty bucks to wash them each week.

Maria was probably in her late thirties or early forties, and she was still kind of hot, but she was completely humorless and had the air of a drill sergeant. She ran a tight ship and ordered Tommy and the rest of us around as if we were in her house and worked for her. We did everything she said even when we didn't understand what she was saying. If it weren't for Maria, Tommy's place would have looked like a pigsty and smelled even worse.

We were young, dumb knuckleheads, most of us longshoremen, who liked to snort blow, drink, and bet. After a weekend with us holding court, Tommy's place smelled like ashtrays, sweat, and stale thrills. If Maria didn't air the place out once a week, I can't imagine how disgusting it would have gotten. We were too busy chasing the rush to care.

One weekend in the fall of 1992, about midway through the college and pro football seasons, Tommy and I were firing on all cylinders when it came to betting. Halfway through a season, the devoted sports bettors start to hit their stride. Since they bet on every game and pay attention to injuries and stats and everything that influences the odds, by midseason they have a real feeling for what is happening in the league. They've got opinions about which teams have juice, and they start to form a picture of how the year is going to play out. Midseason is when I'd get confident and more excited to place bets. There are many reasons to get excited about fall. There's Thanksgiving and nostalgic back-to-school bullshit. If you're a millennial named Amanda, there's the gluten-free pumpkin spice latte at Starbucks. And if you're a degenerate gambler, there's football.

That weekend, Tommy and I and our circle of friends planned accordingly. We got ourselves two eight balls of coke, a case of beer, a bottle of whiskey, and a round of chicken parm heroes. We met at Tommy's apartment and started calling the bookie, placing bets on every single game being played over the next two days. It kicked off with the first college game on Saturday. I hadn't landed my off-campus job yet, so money was tight for me, but that didn't stop me from betting like an economy-class version of Norm Macdonald.

I can't remember all the details, but out of all our friends, Tommy and I were on a roller-coaster run, winning big one game and losing it all the next. We were going bigger than all our friends. We weren't betting the same, so there were times that we were rooting against each other and times that we were on the same side, and the rest of the guys were just the audience. The entire weekend was a nonstop surge fueled by adrenaline, cocaine, and booze. I think the drug dealer came by four times over the course of two days.

All of us were fiends, snorting our drugs through shitty plastic straws that we'd cut with a blunt kitchen knife. The jagged ends tore the inside of our nostrils, and between that, the stepped-on blow we were doing, the cigarettes, and the beer, most of us got nosebleeds some time during the first night game on Saturday. We weren't trying to impress anyone, and we were too high on gambling and drugs to care, plus by then our faces were numb, so we didn't notice the drops of blood falling from our noses all over the couch, the table, and our shirts. Eventually, we got a hand towel and handed it around when one of us needed it, but we weren't too concerned.

After the college games were over Saturday, we went out to a few bars, then split up, planning to get back at it at Tommy's the next day for the NFL games. That Sunday, I won a lot of money on the Giants. I bet the over, and I rarely mixed the over and the Giants line. But I did that day, and I won on both. They were playing the Eagles, their archnemesis, whose quarterback at the time was Randall Cunningham. One of the kids we knew, our quarterback since high school, was a guy named Mike Court, who I'm still friends with today. Mike looks exactly like Randall Cunningham, even more so back then. I'm not exaggerating a bit; it's uncanny. So after partying all day and kind of passing out all over Tommy's apartment, all of us woke up rejuvenated. That is was what I like to call an "inadvertent nap." I woke up in a fantasyland. I think my first words were, "Did the Giants cover?" So, refreshed and regrouped, we decided to go into New York City and take advantage of the bars and clubs that legally remain open until 4:00 a.m.

We ended up at a club called something like Quintessence, which was very bridge and tunnel, and we told every guido and every hot chick that our friend Mike Court was, in fact, Randall Cunningham. Everyone believed us, and by the end of the night, we were running the place. The manager set us up with bottle service, and we had all these girls dancing with us, thinking they were with an NFL quarterback and his friends. Mike was signing autographs. It was amazing.

That is gambling to me. We showed up with nothing, played junk cards, and won. That's no kind of long-term strategy, but that's what keeps me hooked.

Before I finish this story, I'd like to point out that I tried to stop gambling that year, by the way. Tommy and I both did.

I was doing well for myself but not well enough to be betting the way I was, and I loved my mother. I knew I was the provider for us, so I tried to stop. The core nucleus of degenerates was me, Tommy, and another guy, and Tommy backed my idea of cutting out the weekly football wagers. We leaned on each other, pledging that we'd lay off for one entire Sunday-to-Sunday cycle. We talked about it, we got each other excited, even, and like freshly sober people, we got so cocky that we decided we'd watch the games together but not bet. So we met at Tommy's on Sunday and tuned in, and it was eye-opening. There's an old joke about Grateful Dead fans who get sober and realize that they hate the music. The punch line is that they say, "This is what we've been listening to the whole time?"

That's how Tommy and I felt watching the first five seconds of the first NFL game. The kicker punted it, the ball hung in the air, the team ran it back, and by the time one play was over, I felt like I'd aged twenty years. I believe I experienced what people commonly refer to as an epiphany.

"Tommy, you know what?"

"What?

"I've realized something. Without gambling, I hate football."

"You do?"

"Yeah, I do. And you know what else?"

"What?"

"I've realized that I hate you, too."

We both laughed, but I wasn't kidding. If Tommy and I weren't betting, I had very little to talk to him about.

We made it through that awkward Sunday, but we fell off the wagon the very next week. We got together at his place as we always had, neither of us having any intention of betting on any games that weekend. Both of us had kept up a charade of not caring about betting and being enthusiastic about the money we weren't wasting. We cracked a beer and tried to talk about the players and the game as if that was all we needed to enjoy ourselves.

"You know what? Let's go halfway," Tommy said, picking up the newspaper. "I don't even care what the lines are; let's just see."

He turned to the sports pages to find the odds that the betting establishments were giving each team that week. It was the *Daily News* as I remember.

"Eagles are getting 6 . . . Cowboys are getting 4 . . . and the Bills . . . they're getting 8," he said.

This was a season in which the Bills were amazing. Tommy put the paper down. "The Bills getting 8. Yeah, that's a great line," he said. "It's a really great line. But I don't care, because I'm not betting this week. I'm just saying that it's a great line, and all I'm doing is saying to you that they're getting 8."

"You're right; that is a great line," I said. "How great would it be to bet on that . . . I mean, if we were betting. Which we're not."

Listen, Tommy and I were doing our best. We were looking at gambling the way people do when they're trying to question their drinking while drinking a beer. It was a great line; neither of us could deny it.

The moment of silence that filled the room was tremendous.

Then I said, "Did you say what I think you said? The Bills are getting 8?"

"At home."

Two minutes later, we were on the phone to the bookie. Because that year, the Bills at home were unstoppable.

And like that, we were back in it. We lasted one week. If you're a gambler and you see an opportunity like that, you have no choice, so long as you have the ways and means. A great game, with a team at home, getting those kind of points with a home field advantage, there is nothing more exciting to watch on any given Sunday.

Anyway at the end of our banner weekend, after Tommy, Mike, and the rest of our friends had done many bags of cheap coke, drank too much, and somehow faked our way into VIP treatment at Quintessence, I was back at Tommy's apartment, and it was Monday. Somehow, we made it through work and were back to cap things off with Monday Night Football. Thanks to the Giants, I was up $2,000.

Monday was the day that Maria cleaned Tommy's apartment, which she did in the late afternoon, so she was still there when we showed up after work. We were the last degenerates standing, our friends nowhere in sight, and as we settled in to go one last round, Maria was tidying up the fragments of the weekend. Watching her clean up our pizza boxes, beer cans, booze bottles, and overfull ashtrays was sobering. There was a bloody towel, and the stench of exhilaration clung to the walls.

Tommy and I sat on the couch nursing our first beers, talking about the odds on the game while Maria shot us disapproving looks from every corner of the room.

"Who got hurt?" she said, emerging from the bathroom, holding a bloody towel. "And what are these stains on the couch?"

"No one got hurt, Maria," I said. "Don't worry. It's me. I have bad allergies; I got a nosebleed. The neighbor must have a cat. I'm very allergic to dander."

To say that she smirked at me is an understatement. I'd characterize her look as "cynical disgust." The woman had my number the first time I met her.

Ever since I was a kid, I've loved Hawaiian Punch. It has no nutritional value, it's artificial; it's sugar water and empty calories. But it's been my favorite soft drink for as long as I can remember, and it still is. I love it. If I ever go to the gym, I'll bring a water bottle filled with Hawaiian Punch. People who know me associate it with me, because it's my beverage of choice. Frankly, I'm not sure who else besides me even drinks it. When I was on *Stern*, I used to have two or three cans of Hawaiian Punch, a breakfast burrito, and sometimes a cupcake from Crumbs every morning. One time they calculated the calorie intake of my breakfast, and it was something like three thousand, which is one thousand over the suggested two thousand calories that doctors recommend you consume in an entire day. That was just breakfast. I'd usually eat a few hot dogs on my way home, then get dinner later on. Obviously, I was training for the Boston Marathon.

I've always been known for my love of Hawaiian Punch, and since it is bright artificial red, for most of my life, I've also always been known to have Hawaiian Punch stains on my shirts. This isn't a new thing: I used to keep a six-pack of Hawaiian Punch at Tommy's house always, so Maria was well acquainted with the stuff and how often it ended up on my clothes. She'd also found a way to get those stains out of everything. She was a genius.

I was feeling good that evening, because I'd ridden out the insane wave of ups and downs over the course of a volatile weekend. And at that point, going into the final game, I was up $2,000. I think Tommy was even, but both of us were in good spirits and ready to get high one last time and watch the final game of the week.

That is when Maria emerged from the bedroom with a piece of my dirty laundry, a white T-shirt with a prominent dripped stain down the front. It looked like a Jackson Pollock practice run.

Tommy and I were talking about the upcoming game, wondering if we should add a lightning bet before kickoff, when we looked up and saw her.

"This," she said, holding up the shirt. "What is this? Mr. Artie, is it blood or Hawaiian Punch?"

Tommy and I both stared at her for maybe five seconds before we started laughing hysterically. Oddly enough, my roommate and producer, Dan Falato, said the same thing to me just this year. I'm not kidding; he was getting our laundry together for our maid to do and he asked me if a shirt of mine was stained with blood or Hawaiian Punch, because not much has changed in my life. When he said it, neither of us could stop laughing for five minutes.

Maria didn't think it was funny at all. She was annoyed. "This is no funny. Is it blood or Hawaiian Punch? I need to know so I can clean. If it's blood, I clean one way; if Hawaiian Punch, I clean another way."

She started walking toward us, holding up the shirt.

"Maria, wait," I said. "Stay right there." She shot me a look but stopped eight feet away from us.

"What do you think, Tommy?" I asked. "Is that blood or Hawaiian Punch?"

"I think it's blood."

"You do? You sure about that?"

"What do you mean?"

"Are you $2,000 sure that it's blood? It looks like Hawaiian Punch to me."

"Does it?"

"Oh yeah. I'm up $2,000, and I'll bet you everything that it's Hawaiian Punch."

"You're on!" Tommy said. "I say it's blood."

Maria just shook her head.

And there we were, back on the crest of the wave, having the time of our lives.

"Okay, Maria, come here; let's have a look at it."

It was blood. It was clearly blood. It was much too dark to be Hawaiian Punch, a substance whose staining power I had years of experience with. Neither of us batted an eye at how much blood it was, which was a lot.

Tommy won that bet, but he never made me pay up. It's a good thing too. After watching me go from being down $3,000 to being up $2,000 in under forty-eight hours, he was merciful. He never tried to collect, but he's reminded me of his victory for the rest of our lives, so I'm not sure what's worse.

Maria was the one who saw right through me. She was an incredible cleaning woman, but she should have done psychological profiling for the FBI. She went along with everything she witnessed in that apartment but saw it all for what it was. After Tommy was done gloating, Maria came over to me quietly.

"Why did you say Hawaiian Punch?" she asked. "You knew it was blood. I know you know."

There was nothing else to tell her but the truth.

"Because I wanted the action."